SHE IS WORTHY

ENCOUNTERS WITH BIBLICAL WOMEN

Marjorie L. Kimbrough

ABINGDON PRESS

Nashville

SHE IS WORTHY

Copyright © 1994 by Abingdon Press

This book is printed on recycled, acid-free paper.

Library of Congress Cataloging-in-Publication Data

Kimbrough, Marjorie L., 1937–
   She is worthy/by Marjorie L. Kimbrough.
     p.   cm.
   Includes bibliographical references and index.
   ISBN 0-687-00790-9 (pbk.: alk. paper)
    1. Women in the Bible.   2. Self-esteem—Biblical teaching.
  I. Title,
  BS575.K55   1995
  220.9'2'082—dc20
                                  94-37754
                                  CIP

05 06 07 08 09 10 –12 11 10 9

MANUFACTURED IN THE UNITED STATES OF AMERICA

To my friends, Valerie, Sylvia, and Sherry, who each in her own way

is a woman of tremendous self-esteem.

Contents

Introduction

"I think I can; I think I can."

ॐ

*O*ne of the most talked about concepts of modern times is self-esteem. But just what is self-esteem and how long has it been around? Self-esteem is that feeling of self-confidence and self-worth that provides us with the belief in our own ability to reach beyond any limitations or obstacles that might confront us. Essentially, self-esteem encompasses all that we like about ourselves; it is what we think of our ability. If we think we can, then we can. It's like the story of *The Little Engine That Could* whose motto was: "I think I can; I think I can."

As the story goes, other engines that could have taken toys to the girls and boys on the other side of the mountain either thought that they were too important, too busy, too old, or too tired. But one little, blue engine that had never been to the other side of the mountain believed that she could help. As she puffed and chugged she kept saying, "I think I can; I think I can," and she could. The story ends in a roar of cheers for the little engine, and she simply says, "I thought I could; I thought I could."[1] That is what self-esteem is all about. It is wanting to and succeeding because you believe that you can.

A woman of self-esteem values her own worth. She is willing to risk failure, for she knows that no matter what happens, she is still worthy—worthy as a person and therefore worthy to give God praise. God will always welcome her praise and will always value her. She knows this, and this knowledge increases her sense of self-esteem. She is God's child; she is worthy; she can do great things because she is strengthened by her love of self and her love of and devotion to God. She is worthy. *But how many women really believe that? How many women have been raised to believe that? Have you?*

A woman's environment and her surroundings greatly influence her sense of self-esteem. That is why the women of the Bible who had positive self-esteem are so intriguing. So often their family and friends,

---

1. Watty Piper, *The Little Engine That Could* (New York: Platt and Munk, 1961).

their government, and place of worship did little or nothing to support and strengthen their sense of worth; yet, many had it anyway. Many biblical women were able to reach beyond the limits of their environment to touch the hand of God and accomplish tasks previously denied to others. They were not always kind and obedient. Sometimes they were violent and disobedient. But they believed that what they were doing was right because they believed in themselves. By some standards they might be considered failures, but they were often successful because they accomplished what they set out to do. They clearly defined what for them would constitute success in the situation in which they found themselves; they devised a plan of action and they moved forward in faith, knowing that no matter what the outcome, they would still be worthy. This unquestioned sense of self-worth was their spiritual gift from God. They thought they could and they did because they knew that they were persons of value to themselves and to their God.

We build self-esteem through positive reinforcement, and it would have been hard to be a woman of self-esteem during biblical times. Generally, women of biblical times received little positive reinforcement, for most of them were not really considered to be persons of worth. Only men were important; women were merely possessions. Women belonged to their fathers, husbands, brothers, uncles, or some other male relative. They could own no property; they were not considered to be capable of taking care of themselves, and they were often valued only for the dowry they could bring to their father's house.

But was it always like that? Join me as we consider various biblical women. Let us walk through the Bible taking note of various women as we encounter them, and let us seek to discover whether or not they might have been women of self-esteem. We will not always agree with their actions, and we may find that their very sense of self-esteem resulted in false pride, violence, or disobedience; yet, regardless of their actions, I believe that they were women of self-esteem because they retained their sense of self-worth. They had a positive self-image and they believed, although sometimes incorrectly, that the actions they chose were the right ones for the situation in which they found themselves. I ask only that you carefully consider them with me. You may not believe as do I that they were women of self-esteem, but keep in mind the implications of their actions for women of today. *If women of today acted as they did, would you consider these modern women to be women of self-esteem?*

Eve

⊱

Was the first biblical woman, Eve, a woman of self-esteem? Did she have a positive self-image? Did she really like herself? Did she believe that the actions that she chose were the right ones? In the biblical account, God created male and female. The two human creations were given equal appointment to take care of God's creation. They were given specific responsibilities, and they were charged to be obedient. Being aware of this equal appointment and these specific responsibilities would certainly have been a source of self-esteem for Eve. God had created her worthy; she was worthy indeed. Consider Genesis 1:27-28:

> So God created humankind in his image,
> in the image of God he created them;
> male and female he created them.
>
> God blessed them, and God said to them,
> Be fruitful and multiply, and fill the
> earth and subdue it; and have dominion
> over the fish of the sea and over the
> birds of the air and over every living
> thing that moves upon the earth.

Note that God blessed *them* and he charged *them*; In this biblical account, God did not bless the man alone or charge only him. The two whom God created were given everything with only one condition. If they were disobedient, they would suffer the consequences. According to this account, then, Eve knew of her equal responsibility and knew what disobedience would mean. There was only one tree that they were forbidden to touch, and Eve knew what that tree was. In other words, her disobedience was not an accident. She was certainly self-assured and self-confident even though she *was* disobedient. As noted earlier, this may be one characteristic of women of self-esteem. They have so much confidence in themselves that they may fail to be considerate of and obedient to others. They would rather sink or swim on their own; they need neither permission nor instruction. They may even think of themselves as being self-sufficient. There are many indications that the Eve described in this first account is a woman like this. She may have been guilty of false pride. Yet, I still consider this Eve to have been a woman of self-esteem because she never lost her sense of self-worth.

Now, let's consider the second account of the creation. In this account, Genesis 2:7, 16-17, God formed man out of the dust of the ground, and placed him in the Garden of Eden and gave specific instructions to the man, who was alone, not to eat of the tree of the knowledge of good and evil. The responsibility and the consequences were given only to the man. After creating and seeing that all the animals, birds, and fish were named, God created woman.

This latter account portrays woman in a more subservient and observant role, and we can only wonder when and under what circumstances this account was written. We must believe that a man wrote this account since most women were not educated at the time of its writing. If we accept this account as the more accurate one, maybe we can assume that the woman did not know about the conditions of obedience to God; maybe she did not know of her responsibility with regard to her creation. And so, when the woman was beguiled by the serpent, the man blames her. After all, she is his subordinate. He even dares to implicate God by reminding God that God gave the woman to him in the first place.

If we accept this latter account, then Eve is not a woman of self-esteem. She is a forerunner of all women who feel subservient to men. They do not take responsibility for their actions, for they never bother to find out the rules. They simply live day-to-day allowing a man to take care of them, and they quietly accept the blame for all of the failures that the man experiences. They always feel that if they had in some way acted or reacted differently, their man would have succeeded. These are the women that do not know how to take care of the normal responsibilities of running a household, writing checks, and paying bills. If the man in their lives dies, they are lost. The Eve of this account seems to be like this. She has no real sense of self-worth.

But let us go back to the Eve of the first account. That Eve is a woman of self-esteem. She shares equally with her partner, and she knows what directions God has given to both of them. This Eve mistakenly believes that she can outsmart God. So she disobeys God and thinks she'll get away with it. This attitude is so typical of self-assured women. They can outsmart you; they can even charm you into forgetting what it was that you told them not to do. In fact, they can succeed so well at what they were forbidden to do that you will forget that you told them not to do it in the first place. Like Eve, they often put their own plans and wisdom ahead of yours. They may not ever ask permission to do whatever it is that they really want to do because asking gives you the opportunity to tell them no. They do not want to give you that opportunity. *Has this ever happened to you?*

This Eve knew that disobedience applied to her as well as to the man. She also knew the explicit instructions that God gave them. Not only were they not to eat of the forbidden tree, but they were not even to touch it. However, once Eve had assessed the situation, as all women of self-esteem would, she listened to the serpent and decided to eat anyway. Once she had feasted on this delicious, forbidden fruit, she gave to the man, and he ate. Note here that Eve did all the analysis. She heard God give instructions regarding the trees in the garden; she heard the serpent explain the benefits of eating from the forbidden tree; and then she made her own decision. Once her decision had been made, she shared what she had decided with her husband. All he actually did was obey *her*. She offered him the fruit, and he ate. This Eve is really a take-charge person. She is rather bossy, and she orchestrates the disobedience. Women of self-esteem are often bossy and do take charge, but this is because they believe they can do whatever needs to be done. They are easily able to convince others to follow their lead, and Eve convinces Adam.

After having eaten from the tree of the knowledge of good and evil, Adam and Eve discover, and then seek to cover, their nakedness. But note that after they clothe themselves and hide from God, God does not address both the man and the woman; God addresses only the man. It is clear that God holds the man accountable and accuses him of listening to the voice of his wife. It even appears that the man had been impulsive to respond to the whims of a woman.

Consider the order of the conversation: God addresses the man; the man in response addresses God; but the woman addresses God directly without having herself been addressed. To me, this is an act of self-esteem. The woman thinks enough of herself to respond directly to God after she has been blamed by her husband. By placing the blame on her, the husband has given her a role of self-worth, for surely he would not have listened to her or have done what she suggested if he had not had faith in her judgment. All the woman can do at this point to retain her sense of self-esteem is to place the blame on the serpent. At least she has maintained authority over something. Yet, it appears to be at this point that the real subjectivity of the woman occurs. Her former name was woman, taken out of man. Her new name is Eve, meaning life-giving. She will give life, but she will do so in pain. This is a part of her punishment for disobedience. Women of self-esteem, like everyone else, are punished for mistakes. There are no exemptions.

As mother, life-giver, Eve even appears to be somewhat arrogant. She believes that she is like God. She can give life, and she is typical of other self-assured women who often appear arrogant. Consider the name of her first born, Cain, meaning gotten or acquired. She got a son; she did it on her own. But what of the second born, Abel, whose name means breath. Perhaps by the time Abel was born, Eve realized that life is but a breath that can be snuffed out at any moment, especially if sin is involved. Maybe she is not like God after all, for sin did play a part in ending Abel's life. His brother killed him, and Eve experienced the heartache and pain that resides with all other mothers of sinful children. God does have a way of reminding us that we are only human.

As a woman of self-esteem, Eve learned from her experiences, and she was blessed with a third son, Seth. His name means to appoint or to establish, for God appointed him to replace the son she had lost, and it was from his seed that Jesus is traced.[2]
Eve is also a grandmother to Enoch, and what grandmother have we ever met who was not proud and self-assured, showing us pictures of her grandchild. Yes, I believe Eve qualifies as a biblical woman of self-esteem.

2. Edith Deen, *All of the Women of the Bible* (San Francisco: HarperCollins, 1988), p. 7.

Sarah

ぞ⋗

Sarah is one of the most intriguing women of the Bible.
She must have been very beautiful, for her husband found it
necessary to pass her off as his sister so that no one would kill
him in order to have her (Genesis 12:10-20). Her husband,
Abraham, even said to her, "I know well that you are a woman
beautiful in appearance" (Genesis 12:11). Just imagine a
woman of biblical times hearing her husband offer her this
kind of flattering praise. This alone would have been sufficient
to build her self-esteem.

It must have been true in biblical times, even as it is today,
that beauty was a commodity greatly treasured. Most biblical
women of self-esteem were identified as very beautiful no matter
what other attributes they were given. Sarah, then, being a
woman of great self-confidence and self-esteem, did what was
necessary to save her husband—even if it meant putting herself
in jeopardy. She did what was expected of a beautiful, obedient
wife. The biblical account provides us no evidence that she was
unwilling to be taken into the house of the Egyptian pharaoh and
because of her, the pharaoh richly rewarded Abraham with
"sheep, oxen, male donkeys, male and female slaves, female
donkeys, and camels" (Genesis 12:16). Thus, as Abraham had
predicted, her actions had made things better for him and
knowing this, her sense of self-worth must have been enhanced.
Sarah might even have remained with the pharaoh had not the
Lord "afflicted Pharaoh and his house with great plagues"
because of his displeasure with this deception (Genesis 12:17).

Without hesitation, the pharaoh sent Abraham "on the way, with his wife and all that he had" (Genesis 12:20*b*).

Now, while Sarah had her beauty and her position as the wife of a very wealthy man, she lacked the one thing that would have completed her status as a biblical woman of self-esteem. She had no children. A less self-assured woman might have quietly accepted her barren state, but Sarah was very sure of herself, and she was willing to use everything she had, including her servants, to secure the fulfillment of God's promise to her husband. And so, the self-assured, self-confident Sarah initiated the first case of surrogate parenting, and then, as now, the situation caused more problems than it solved.

Sarah offered Hagar, her servant, as the vehicle for the fulfillment of God's promise that Abraham should be the father of nations. No thought was given to Hagar as a person; she was simply offered as a slave to do her mistress or master's bidding. Hagar complied and conceived. The fact that she was able to conceive raised her own level of self-esteem because in biblical times a woman who was blessed with children was to be respected. Thus, there was conflict between the two women who up until this point had no reason to be in conflict. The lines that separated them were clear—maid and mistress. With the conception, the lines became fuzzy. We had a woman blessed with fertility and one cursed with barrenness. The maid had come to view herself as superior to her mistress, and the mistress could not tolerate this attitude. To preserve her own dignity and sense of self-worth, Sarah had to get rid of Hagar whose very presence was a constant reminder of her own failure as a woman.

Sarah approached Abraham and asked him to get rid of Hagar. (Now this is where I personally lose all respect for Abraham who had impregnated Hagar but did not in any way seek to protect her.) Abraham simply told Sarah to do with Hagar whatever she would. This was an empowering act for Sarah, and it served to build her self-esteem. She was able to dismiss from her presence the woman who carried the child who was to be her husband's heir. Sarah used the power given her, and dealt so harshly with Hagar that she ran away. But Hagar returned to Sarah's household at the urging of the angel of the Lord, and this return must have served to elevate Sarah's self-esteem even more. I can just hear Sarah saying, "No matter how I treat her she returns, for life in my household is better than life anywhere else."

Eventually Sarah received the crowning blessing that assured her self-worth. She became pregnant in her old age and bore a son, Isaac. One might think that Sarah would have no further reason to assert herself, but she did. Sarah was very protective of her son's inheritance, and asked Abraham to cast out both Hagar and the son she bore. Although the Bible records that Abraham was distressed by this request, he abided by Sarah's wishes and Hagar and her son were sent away. Sarah's self-esteem was intact, for she had her husband and his son in position for the fulfillment of God's promise.

And how typical is Sarah of women whom we might encounter today? Was her sense of self-esteem threatened by Hagar and the son, the first-born son, that she bore? *Would you be threatened by one who had borne your husband's first child?* Sarah was willing to take no chances, and she was in the position to do what modern women might only dream of. She sent her competition away.

But God remembered Hagar and her son, for God had promised that through her son, Ishmael, a great nation would be born (Genesis 21:13, 18-21). So, they did not die in the wilderness. They traveled on to Arabia, and many years later, in year A.D. 570, Muhammad, the founder of Islam, the apostle of Allah, and a descendent of Hagar's son Ishmael, was born.[3]

God's promise that Abraham would be the father of nations did not exclude the possibility that he would be the father of more than one great nation through more than one son. Knowing that God would fulfill his promise to her must have given Hagar a measure of self-esteem. That's an interesting thing about self-esteem—one person can not have it all!

---

3. W. Gunther Plaut, *The Torah* (New York: Union of American Hebrew Congregations, 1981), p. 139.

Leah

&❧

*L*eah may seem to be an unlikely candidate for a woman of self-esteem, but let us look closely at her life. Leah was the older of Laban's two daughters (the other's name was Rachel), and Leah was not the prettier. It is said that "Leah's eyes were lovely, and Rachel was graceful and beautiful" (Genesis 29:17). As we look closely at the Hebrew word that in this verse has been translated as 'lovely,' we find that the word may actually mean 'weak' or 'dull.' These, perhaps even sad, eyes were not necessarily attractive to men who preferred bright, exciting eyes, the kind of eyes that Rachel had. Just consider Jacob's reaction when he first met Rachel who, described as beautiful, he greeted with a kiss. Jacob's attraction to Rachel was immediate and lasting. If ever there was a case of love at first sight, this was surely it.

But what of Leah? She must have seen the reaction of Jacob to her sister. She was even probably accustomed to men looking past her at her younger sister, but Leah was not discouraged. She knew her time would come. She watched as Jacob made a bargain with her father, Laban, to work for seven years in exchange for the hand of Rachel in marriage. She was well aware that it was not customary for the younger sister to marry before the older, but Leah was a proud woman of self-esteem, and she would not begrudge her sister the fulfillment that so great a love would bring. Everyone around must have heard Jacob say that the seven years "seemed to him but a few days because of the love he had for her" (Genesis 29:20*b*). How Leah must have longed for some man to say those words in response to his love for her.

So when the time for the marriage had come, Leah prepared along with her sister to attend the feast. She, as would any woman of self-esteem, wished for her sister every happiness. But Leah was an obedient daughter, and when her father told her that she—not her sister—would enter the marriage tent, Leah complied. Laban had deceived Jacob, and he had used his daughter as a partner. There must have been a hint of deception running through the family, for Laban's sister Rebekah (Jacob's mother) had helped Jacob to deceive his father Isaac and thereby gain the blessing from his older brother Esau. In this instance Laban is helping his daughter take the intended husband of her sister.

Leah was forced to enter into a marriage with a man she knew to be in love with her sister. Can you imagine this? *What would you do?* Leah accepted her fate, loved the husband, and hoped that someday he would return her love. She made the best of the situation at hand. Jacob was probably a very handsome man, and Leah was confident that she could make him happy, for she knew that she would be a wonderful, faithful wife, worthy of adoration and love. Perhaps Leah did not count on Jacob's willingness to work another seven years for her sister Rachel. Leah probably would not have planned to share her husband with her sister, but that was her fate, and she accepted it.

What would a proud woman of self-esteem do when faced with a husband who loved his other wife, her sister, more? She would seek to make him a proud and devoted father and in that way gain his love. With her plan in mind, Leah prayed that God would bless her with children. Women of self-esteem never yield to the feeling of defeat, and they rely on God for sustenance. God heard her prayer. "When the LORD saw that Leah was unloved, he opened her womb; but Rachel was barren. Leah conceived and bore a son, and she named him Reuben; for she said, 'Because the LORD has looked on my affliction; surely now my husband will love me'" (Genesis 29:31-32). The ever confident Leah believed that this son whom she bore and named to signify her sense of being blessed with a son and remembered by God, would win for her the love of her husband. *You might know how difficult it is to be the bearer of unrequited love.* But Leah did not give up.

She conceived again and bore a son she named Simeon which meant God had heard or remembered her continuing cry. She felt hated, but God loved her. Leah was blessed with a third son, Levi. His name was symbolic of her attachment to her husband. Levi means attached or joined, and through this attachment, Leah was not only joined to her husband but to all future generations of Jews. Moses, the giver of the Law, the great prophet of Judaism, descends from the line of Levi (Exodus 6:16-18, 20). And then Leah conceived again, and bore a son Judah whose name meant "praise the LORD." Leah had finally realized that God is the source of all joy whether her husband ever loved her or not. And from this line, the line of the son with the name of praise, Jesus descends (Matthew 1:2-16; Luke 3:23, 31-33). Thus Leah, the woman who believed in herself and in her ability to be loved, connected the promise given to Abraham with both the Jews and the Christians. She was a woman truly blessed.

But women of self-esteem never quit, and Leah, even after having been blessed with four fine sons, still wanted to win Jacob's love. It appears that after the birth of Judah, Jacob no longer visited Leah's tent, for she had stopped conceiving. And having already been blessed with four sons, he was content to sleep with Rachel, the woman whom he loved best even though she was barren. In an attempt to win Jacob back, Leah carefully watched her sister and copied her actions. Rachel had given Jacob her maid to act as a surrogate mother. Rachel's maid bore Jacob two sons, so Leah gave Jacob her maid, and she also bore Jacob two sons. Leah named the sons her maid bore, Gad, meaning good fortune, and Asher, meaning happy. These two new sons added to Leah's good fortune and happiness.

Still Leah persisted. She never would stop trying to win Jacob's love. When her son Reuben found mandrakes, a fruit believed to have powers of fertility, Rachel asked for some. Leah saw this request as an opportunity to welcome Jacob back to her tent. So she said, "'Is it a small matter that you have taken away my husband? Would you take away my son's mandrakes also?' Rachel said, 'Then he may lie with you tonight for your son's mandrakes'" (Genesis 30:15). Leah had purchased the right to have Jacob return to her, and she intended to shower him with love. When Jacob came in from the field, she greeted him with the outcome of her bargain. She even told him that she had hired him, and the son that she conceived as a result of that encounter she named Issachar meaning God has given me my hire.

Seeing that Leah was able to conceive again, Jacob slept with her additional nights, and she bore him another son, Zebulun, meaning good dowry. She said, "God has endowed me with a good dowry; now my husband will honor me, because I have borne him six sons" (Genesis 30:20). The last child that Leah bore Jacob was his only daughter whom she named Dinah. Although no particular meaning is given to her name, she is the first biblical daughter whose name is recorded at birth.

Leah found comfort in being able to love Jacob and to bear his children. She realized that his devotion to her sister was too strong to break, but she at least wanted the opportunity to share in loving their husband. And perhaps the fertility powers associated with the mandrakes that she had used to bargain with Rachel actually worked, for God remembered Rachel and she bore Jacob two sons, Joseph and Benjamin. However, regrettably Rachel became the first recorded biblical woman to die in childbirth.

So, ultimately Leah's ability to accept her second place status with her husband, to remain faithful and loving, and to persist in seeking to win his love and favor without losing her sense of self-worth was rewarded. For, after her sister's death she could become his sole source of comfort and she alone could occupy the primary place next to her husband. She had, in all likelihood even before her marriage, loved him with the unconditional love that he had reserved for her sister. She knew that his loving her sister did not make her less of a woman; all she wanted was the opportunity to show that she loved him more than anyone else. The names of her sons said it all. She was blessed of God; she praised God; she had good fortune, she was happy; and she was richly endowed. She was a woman of self-esteem!

Jochebed

ða

*J*ochebed was surely a mother of tremendous self-esteem. She knew what she had to do to protect her son's life, and she did it without hesitation. Her plan even involved risking his precious life in order to save it.

Can you imagine a mother placing her newborn infant in a basket in the Nile River and leaving a child to watch? Although she had carefully treated the basket with bitumen and pitch (Exodus 2:3) to waterproof it, suppose the basket had started to sink or suppose the child left to watch had fallen asleep? What would Jochebed have done? *What would you have done?* How would she have explained her seemingly careless and irresponsible action to her husband? How would she have lived with herself? *How would you have lived with yourself?* Remember, this mother was a woman of tremendous self-esteem, and women of self-esteem are so sure of success that they are willing to take risks. And aren't we glad that Jochebed did?

Although Jochebed was well aware that the Egyptian pharaoh had ordered that all male babies be killed, it seems to me that she must have been a religious woman whom God had informed of a special purpose for her male child. So with God's help, Jochebed devised her plan. She kept her eyes and ears open and waited for God to make clear to her what she was to do. During this waiting and planning phase, she managed to hide her baby for three months. By the end of the three months she knew what she had to do.

I wonder how often we jump into a life-challenging situation without waiting to hear from the Lord? Women of self-esteem are often led to listen, wait, and meditate until God directs them, for somehow they know that God will guide and instruct them if they but patiently wait. It takes assurance and self-confidence to successfully wait on the Lord. Jochebed had it.

God directed her to observe the bathing patterns of the pharaoh's daughter. God revealed to her the way to coach her daughter, Miriam, so that Miriam would know what to say and do when the pharaoh's daughter appeared. God demonstrated to her the way to construct and waterproof the baby's basket, and God showed her where to hide her daughter so that she had full view of the basket and the activity surrounding it.

Jochebed's sense of self-worth did not stop with herself. It extended to her daughter also, for she was convinced that she had raised Miriam to be responsible enough not to take her eyes off her brother or the basket. Somehow Jochebed knew that if anything went amiss, Miriam would find her.

Once Jochebed was convinced that Miriam knew exactly what to do, she was able to let go of her beloved child and let God and her daughter do what she knew they would. *How often do you dare to let go and let God and God's appointed servants do their jobs?* If Jochebed had been around and been seen by one of the maids, the whole plan might have fallen apart. But Jochebed was a woman of self-esteem, and she was convinced that God's plan for her son would be fulfilled. And it was!

The baby was discovered, the appropriate nurse was summoned, and Jochebed had the opportunity to raise her own child and be paid for doing it. Just imagine Jochebed's joy at being able to watch her child grow up while having the opportunity to instill in him her own Hebrew values and faith in God. Jochebed's unselfish willingness to submit to God's direction was rewarded, for although her son was raised in luxury as the son of the pharaoh's daughter, he never forgot either his Hebrew tradition or the values that made him a great leader.

God's plan came together for this wonderful Hebrew woman of tremendous self-esteem, and Moses, the giver of the Law, the great Hebrew prophet, was saved! Thanks be to God for this mother and her self-esteem!

Miriam

ও

S he was a sister, a prophetess, a nationalist, and a leader of praise. She was also a woman of self-esteem. We first met Miriam as she was charged with the responsibility of watching over the infant brother who was slated to be killed along with all the other male Hebrew babies. But Miriam was equal to the task for she had been raised by Jochebed, a courageous woman of self-esteem, and she had learned well. Although she only spoke one sentence in our first encounter with her, that sentence represented a turning point for all her people. Responding to her mother's coaching, she boldly asked the pharaoh's daughter, "Shall I go and get you a nurse from the Hebrew women to nurse the child for you?" (Exodus 2:7). Thus, because she assertively helped to save her brother, all of her people would one day be free from their fate of bondage in Egypt.

There is no record of Miriam's ever having married, so it appears that she was one of the first biblical women to have had interests beyond the home. She does not appear to have been preoccupied with finding a husband or fulfilling her calling to motherhood. She was interested in tribal affairs. She was with her people as they traveled through the wilderness, and she was there to lead them as they crossed the Red Sea. *Have you ever felt called in a direction different from the one people expect of you? How have you responded?*

Once they were successfully across the sea, the prophet Moses sang a song of praise and thanksgiving to God that was also intended for the benefit of the people, but the prophetess Miriam led the women in song and praise. Moses may have been the stoic, stilted preacher who expected the people to quietly listen to his sermon, but Miriam was the enthusiastic worship leader who expected the people to join her in praise. She wanted tambourines and dancing, and her song reflected that. While Moses began his song, "I will sing to the LORD" (Exodus 15:1a), Miriam included all by saying, "Sing [everyone] to the LORD, for he has triumphed gloriously; horse and rider he has thrown into the sea" (Exodus 15:21). It is clear that brother and sister were leaders of different styles, and this difference caused conflict in the years that followed.

As a woman of self-esteem, Miriam found it difficult to share leadership, and unfortunately, she fell victim to envy. Disturbed because Moses had married a woman from an idolatrous country, Miriam said to Aaron, "Has the LORD spoken only through Moses? Has he not spoken through us also?" (Numbers 12:2). Although Moses was unquestionably the recognized leader, his siblings, Miriam and Aaron, felt equally called of God. It appeared that Moses may not even have been as faithful to God as they had, for he had married outside the faith. Miriam, being the proud woman that she was and having sought leadership rather than the typical home and family, wanted the people to listen to her as well. But God made the difference between the three clear by saying:

Hear my words:
When there are prophets among
  you,
 I the LORD make myself
  known to them in visions;
 I speak to them in dreams.
Not so with my servant Moses;
 he is entrusted with all my
  house.
With him I speak face to face—
 clearly, not in riddles;
 and he beholds the form of the
  LORD.
Why then were you not afraid to speak against my servant Moses?
(Numbers 12:6-8)

Moses was not like any other prophet; he had beheld the face of God. Miriam and Aaron were ordinary prophets who only saw visions. They had no right to criticize Moses, and God was angry with them.

Miriam caught the brunt of God's anger, for she was stricken with leprosy. To secure her healing it took the pleading of both her brothers—Aaron to Moses and Moses to God. Moses understood her frustration and forgave her in love. God did not deny Moses. God promised to heal Miriam, but allowed her seven days outside the camp of the people to consider and reconsider her criticism of God's chosen prophet. But Miriam obviously had influence because "the people did not set out on the march until Miriam had been brought in again." (Numbers 12:15b)

Moses and Miriam were loyal and faithful servants of God. Miriam understood total praise with the whole body. Her style of praise may have been too loud and enthusiastic for Moses who wanted everyone to be still and know God. The two conflicted in both worship and leadership styles, but God used them both. Miriam did not get to the promised land with the people, but her song of praise did. Through it she lives on!

Deborah

ะ

*D*eborah's story is recorded in the book of Judges, chapters 4 and 5, and because of this placement, we are assured that Deborah is remembered as a judge. Not only is she the first judge mentioned, but she is also the only female judge, and this unique position must have given her the kind of confidence that made her a woman of self-esteem. The people of Israel obviously saw something special and unique about Deborah to have placed her in this political position of honor. They formed a constant procession seeking her advice and counsel while she calmly sat under the palm tree in the hill country of Ephraim. Deborah was bright and prophetic. The advice she dispensed was well received, and because her prophecies proved to be true, she was called a prophetess.

We know that Deborah was married, for her husband, Lappidoth, is identified in the same Bible verse that introduces her (Judges 4:4). We notice right away that in this introduction Deborah is identified as a prophetess, judge of Israel, and the wife of Lappidoth. Even though the entire verse is about Deborah, she is called Lappidoth's wife. Although it appears that a more meaningful identification would have been to label him as her husband, the worth attributed to men was so great during this time period that it probably would have been insulting to suggest in any way that a man belonged to a woman. Nevertheless, Lappidoth is only presented as a background character, for he is not mentioned again. Deborah is the important character, and she is credited with having positions of worth in Israel—wife, prophetess, and judge. She is presented as a powerful leader, a woman of self-esteem who can summon men at her will. And that is exactly what she did.

Israel had been asleep for far too long. Deborah knew that the time had come to wake the country up. This knowledge had come to her as a part of her prophetic perception. The Canaanites had oppressed the Israelites for more than twenty years. The Canaanites had over nine hundred chariots of iron and Israel had none, yet Deborah knew that it was her responsibility to inform Israel that God would deliver them, chariots or not. Like so many other women of self-esteem, Deborah had faith. The God she served was able, and she took it upon herself to inform her constituents.

Deborah summoned Barak, a member of the tribe of Naphtali, to be the leader of the Israelites as they engaged in what she knew would be the defeat of Sisera, the Canaanite general. Speaking as a prophetess, Deborah told Barak what the Lord, not she, had commanded. She instructed him to take ten thousand men from the Israelite tribes, and to await the delivery of Sisera into his hands.

Even though Deborah had spoken and prophesied with the conviction of a woman of tremendous self-esteem, Barak refused to go into battle without her. He said to her, "If you will go with me, I will go; but if you will not go with me, I will not go" (Judges 4:8). Barak was smart enough to realize that all of the instructions for the victory were being given to Deborah, so he did not want to venture out without her. Barak needed her prophetic skills to let him know how and when the victory would be realized. *I wonder how many men today recognize the strength and courage that can be gained from partnership with a woman of self-esteem?*

Barak certainly understood the value of a woman of self-esteem, and he was rewarded, for Deborah responded, "I will surely go with you; nevertheless, the road on which you are going will not lead to your glory, for the LORD will sell Sisera into the hand of a woman" (Judges 4:9a). With this positive response, Barak learned even more than he had bargained for. He had expected to learn where the victory would take place, but he did not expect to learn how. It certainly came as a surprise to him that another woman would figure into the plans. This was the prophecy Deborah foretold. Barak accepted the prophecy and proceeded to carry it out. He summoned the ten thousand warriors to accompany them as Deborah had instructed, and then the two of them led the warriors forward to defeat the enemy.

When Sisera learned that Barak was preparing for battle, he gathered his chariots and his troops and went to meet the enemy. But Deborah fulfilled her role as prophetess, for she let Barak know that God would deliver Sisera. She said, "Up! For this is the day on which the LORD has given Sisera into your hand. The LORD is indeed going out before you" (Judges 4:14). And the Lord did deliver as promised, for the very sight of Barak and his ten thousand men threw Sisera into chaos resulting in his desertion of his troops and the destruction of all who remained.

Sisera's flight led him right into the arms of the one who would slay him, for he found the tent of Heber the Kenite who had separated his tent from the other members of his tribe. Upon seeing this lone tent, I am sure that Sisera thought that he had found a safe haven. Jael, Heber's wife, greeted Sisera with warm and comforting hospitality. She encouraged him to enter her tent and take refuge, for he would be safe with her. She even covered him up and served him warm milk.

Consider the predicament Sisera faced. He had abandoned his troops; he did not know how far the enemy was behind him, and he was cold and hungry. He was warmly greeted by a woman who said that he would be safe in her tent; she offered cover for his cold body; and, although he had only asked for water, she had provided milk. What more could he want? How could he refuse? I see this woman as suddenly becoming the mother he needed when he was feeling defeated. She had offered him a blanket of security and she had offered him milk. She must have seemed trustworthy, for she was surrounded with those symbols of maternal care. So he accepted her hospitality, her mothering, and while he was sleeping, she killed him.

Jael had become the woman whom Deborah prophesied would deliver Sisera. She, like Deborah, had to have been a woman of considerable self-esteem and confidence. Jael had been able to competently convince a Canaanite general that she could provide him safety. She knew that she had to succeed in deceiving him with warmth and nourishment, and she had to believe that she was strong enough to kill him by driving a tent peg through his temple. Although her actions resulted in violence, she felt that she was doing the will of God. She was quite a woman of self-esteem and as such she believed in demonstrating her worth, for she felt that she had to deliver just as Deborah had predicted. *Could you perform violent actions if you believed you were doing God's will? Do you think violence is ever God's will?*

Jael had even appeared to have gone along with Sisera's instructions to deny having seen him, for he felt secure enough to fall asleep. Having accomplished her task, Jael proceeded to greet Barak who had been in pursuit of Sisera, and she was able to inform him that his enemy was dead.

The Canaanites were defeated just as Deborah had predicted, and the Song of Deborah (Judges 5) offers all praise to God. The song also speaks of Deborah as a mother in Israel who had to awaken the sleeping children to action, to trust in God, and to awareness that God would keep them in peace. Deborah was honored, she was called the most worthy of all names, "mother," and she was a woman of great self-esteem.

Samson's Mother

૨&

*I*dentified only as Manoah's wife or as Samson's mother, I see her as a woman of self-esteem. She lived during the time that the Israelites had been delivered into the hands of the Philistines because they had done what was evil in the sight of the Lord. She was destined to bear the child who would begin their rescue.

Manoah's wife suffered from the same fate that seemed to have plagued many of those who had the ability to be great mothers; she was barren. But God looked on her condition, and sent his angel to inform her of the tremendous blessing that was in store. The angel said to her: "Although you are barren, having borne no children, you shall conceive and bear a son. Now be careful not to drink wine or strong drink, or to eat anything unclean, for you shall conceive and bear a son. No razor is to come on his head, for the boy shall be a nazirite to God from birth. It is he who shall begin to deliver Israel from the hand of the Philistines" (Judges 13:3-5). Imagine the joy that Manoah's wife must have felt. She would not only bear a treasured male child, but that child would be identified as one dedicated to the service of God, the sacred calling of a nazirite. He would have the outwardly visible symbol of his calling—long, uncut hair. Everyone would know that he was God's child.

Rushing to share her good news with her husband, Manoah's wife found him to be somewhat skeptical of her information. He did not believe her or trust her authority. He wanted to hear exactly what had been said and instructed. He probably thought that his wife had not gotten the message straight, so he prayed that God would send his messenger to them, both of them, again. But God had identified Manoah's wife as a woman of self-esteem, one who understood her worth, and there was no need to send the angel to both of them. Again, God sent the angel to Manoah's wife while she sat alone. This time Manoah's wife ran to get her husband. She knew that he was the type of man who needed to see the angel for himself, and she did not want to miss her blessing because of a doubting husband. As a woman of self-esteem, she also possessed the quality of understanding what her husband needed. Seeking to fulfill his need did not diminish her in the least.

Manoah's wife greeted her husband with the words, "The man who came to me the other day has appeared to me" (Judges 13:10). Following his wife to the place where the man was, Manoah asked, "Are you the man who spoke to this woman?" (Judges 13:11). Somehow Manoah still did not believe the words of a woman. He wanted verification from a man. But God did not need to verify his blessing to Manoah. The person who needed the instructions had already gotten them. The angel simply told Manoah to have his wife observe everything that she had been told. Manoah would have to trust his wife. He would have to learn that God speaks to women as well as to men. She knew what to do. She had perceived the meaning of the message even though he had not. She was a woman of self-esteem. All her husband had to do was allow her to do what she had been told.

Manoah wanted to detain the angel, for he still needed to be convinced of the truth of the blessing. He offered to prepare him a meal, but the angel told him to offer the food as a sacrifice, a burnt offering in praise of God. As the burnt offering along with a grain offering were being made, the angel ascended to the heavens in the flame right before the eyes of Manoah and his wife, and the two of them fell face down to the ground. With this turn of events, Manoah was finally convinced that they had been in the presence of the angel of the Lord. He said, "We shall surely die, for we have seen God" (Judges 13:22). This statement further demonstrated Manoah's lack of understanding, but our woman of self-esteem set him straight. She said, "If the LORD had meant to kill us, he would not have accepted a burnt offering and a grain offering at our hands, or shown us all these things, or now announced to us such things as these" (Judges 13:23). She was convinced that God was blessing them, and she was prepared to move forward observing the instructions she had been given.

Manoah's wife gave birth to Samson, and she did not cut his hair. She raised him to drink no wine or strong drink and to eat no unclean food. But no matter how hard good mothers try, sometimes their children disobey. *Think of a time when your child or someone in your charge disobeyed, despite your best efforts. How was your self-esteem affected?* Samson was no exception. He violated his mother's training, and he sought to marry one of the Philistine women. His mother objected to his marriage to one who did not worship God. Remembering that he was destined to begin the deliverance of their people from the hand of the Philistines, she wondered how this marriage could bring anything but evil. She and Manoah said to him, "Is there not a woman among your kin, or among all our people, that you must go to take a wife from the uncircumcised Philistines?" (Judges 14:3). But as are many young men, Samson was obsessed with the woman's beautiful appearance. He said, "Get her for me, because she pleases me" (Judges 14:3b).

Samson's mother did not realize that it would be through this marriage that God would begin to work out the deliverance of the Israelites. It was Samson's alliance with Delilah after his bride was killed that led to his violation of the vows promised by his mother before his birth. This violation, the cutting of his hair, led to his capture, but his capture led to his destruction of the Philistines. His mother's rearing gave him the strength to endure and deliver his people—even if it meant his life. He is remembered by the writer of Hebrews when his name is called along with others "who through faith conquered kingdoms, administered justice, obtained promises, shut the mouths of lions, quenched raging fire, escaped the edge of the sword, won strength out of weakness, became mighty in war, put foreign armies to flight" (Hebrews 11:33-34).

Before his birth, when Samson's mother repeated the words of the angel to her husband, she had said, "the boy shall be a nazirite to God from birth to the day of his death" (Judges 13:7b). The angel had simply said to her, "the boy shall be a nazirite to God from birth" (Judges 13:5a). Somehow Samson's mother had seen the day of his death along with the blessing of his birth. Yet, she had the strength to follow the instructions given her and raise her son in the faith. She was a strong woman. She was a woman of faith and obedience to God. Her son began the deliverance of her people, the Israelites, from the hand of the Philistines. She was a woman of self-esteem!

Ruth

இ

W hat is it about Ruth that would make one consider her to be a woman of self-esteem? Well, she believed in herself, and successful people of self-esteem do that. She believed that she and her mother-in-law could make it in a man's world without a man, which demonstrates that she believed in her worth as a person. After the deaths of her father-in-law, her brother-in-law, and her husband, she refused to take the easy way out and return to the safety of her homeland. She was willing to take a risk on her surviving in a strange land with strange people. If she had returned to her people in the land of Moab, she could have had an easy life. Undoubtedly there were male relatives who would have taken responsibility for her; after all, she had been a faithful wife for ten years and that attribute certainly would have been appealing. But Ruth's idea of success and self-esteem was not tied to the land of Moab.

Her mother-in-law, Naomi, encouraged her to go home. Naomi even insisted that she had no more sons for either Ruth or her other daughter-in-law, Orpah, to marry. Naomi offered further words of discouragement when she said, "Turn back, my daughters, go your way, for I am too old to have a husband. Even if I thought there was hope for me, even if I should have a husband tonight and bear sons, would you then wait until they were grown?" (Ruth 1:12-13a). It appears from this testimony that Naomi's concept of security and self-esteem was related to marriage and the family. She could not conceive of a full and successful life without a husband, and although she felt that her time for such a life had passed, she wanted it for her daughters-in-law. While Naomi's words persuaded Orpah to return to her own people, Ruth decided to take on the responsibility of providing for herself and her mother-in-law. She was convinced that she could do it. Ruth was confident. She had self-esteem.

The bond between mother-in-law and daughter-in-law must have been great indeed. Naomi's husband had died shortly after the journey to Moab, and Naomi had been a part of her sons' household for ten years. The close mother-to-family relationship is noted in Naomi's telling her daughters-in-law to return to their mother's house (Ruth 1:8). We might have expected Naomi to say "father's house," but the mother bond is so real in their relationships that she was compelled to say "mother's house." We do not know the whole story here. Perhaps so many men in the land of Moab had died during this time period (we certainly know that the three men in Naomi's family had), that many houses were the mother's house. At least I am convinced that the loyalty of Ruth to Naomi was real, and Naomi saw herself as Ruth's mother, one who no longer had a house to offer her. Thus she was sending Ruth to her other mother's house.

The words used in response to Naomi's insistence that Ruth return to Moab have been repeated for many years in wedding ceremonies and other pledges of faith and loyalty. Consider the power of the words: "Do not press me to leave you or to turn back from following you! Where you go, I will go; where you lodge, I will lodge; your people shall be my people; and your God my God. Where you die, I will die—there will I be buried. May the LORD do thus and so to me, and more as well, if even death parts me from you" (Ruth 1:16-17). These are powerful words and they exemplify the depth of the commitment between the two women. It takes real self-esteem to make this type of commitment. One who is willing to leave the security of one's own people, pledge to worship another God, and even be buried in foreign soil must be both secure and confident. Ruth was. *Are you? Could you be? Would you want to be?*

And so Naomi accepted the challenge that Ruth offered and invited her along on the return to Bethlehem. You can only imagine the talk caused by the sight of these two women returning alone. Naomi even felt compelled to respond by telling everyone to call her by a new name. She had left full, with husband and sons, and she had returned empty, with only a daughter-in-law. We readily see that Naomi's sense of worth and self-esteem was tied to her having a husband and sons; she felt empty without them.

But it is Ruth who took the initiative. Ruth asked Naomi's permission to glean in the fields hoping that she would be noticed and find favor with one who could help her achieve her goal of providing for herself and her mother-in-law. Because Ruth was a woman of self-esteem, she did not just go into the fields with hope alone; she actively worked to achieve her goal. Ruth must have dressed and conducted herself in a manner that made her stand out, for Boaz noticed her and inquired as to whom she belonged. The response he got also lets us know that Ruth was serious. Boaz was informed by his servant that after having asked permission to glean behind the reapers, Ruth had, in his own words, "been on her feet from early this morning until now, without resting even for a moment" (Ruth 2:7*b*). This had to have been impressive. And Boaz was impressed. He paved the way for her to glean as much as she needed; he told her to stay close to the young women; he told the young men to leave her alone; and he even offered her some of his bread and wine. Ruth was well on her way to accomplishing her goal of surviving in a foreign land.

When Ruth returned with her great bounty, Naomi asked where she had gleaned. Upon learning that it was in Boaz's field, Naomi responded, "The man is a relative of ours, one of our nearest kin" (Ruth 2:20*b*). This response again affirms the close relationship between the two women. Boaz is their relative, not just Naomi's. It was at this point that Naomi began to put into action her plan to help Ruth achieve the success and security they both needed. As we might already suspect, Naomi's plan would necessarily involve marriage and the family, for this was where her definition of success and security was based.

Although Ruth was convinced that she could continue with her daily gleaning in the fields thus providing for herself and her mother-in-law, Naomi had more ambitious plans. Ruth was secure enough to obey her mother-in-law's direction. Because Naomi felt the most security in a marriage with children, she desired the same for Ruth. She carefully plotted her strategy, beginning with instructions for Ruth to anoint and adorn herself in her finest and present herself to Boaz for the taking. Although Naomi believed that Boaz would take the initiative in this situation and instructed Ruth that he would tell her what to do, it was in fact actually Ruth, our woman of self-esteem, who took the initiative and told Boaz what to do. She told him to spread his cloak over her, for he was the next of kin (Ruth 3:9). He followed her direction and she stayed with him until the next morning.

Boaz had committed himself to Ruth, and he had to determine if there was anyone who had a greater claim to her than he did. In fact, there was actually a kinsman who could have claimed Ruth and all that had belonged to Naomi's husband and sons, but he relinquished his right to Boaz. Thus, Ruth's goal of successfully providing for herself and her mother-in-law was accomplished. She married Boaz and bore a son. But the interesting thing is that Naomi became the child's nurse, for she needed that child in order to feel full. The scripture even says, "The women of the neighborhood gave him a name, saying, 'A son has been born to Naomi'" (Ruth 4:17*a*). But Ruth was strong enough to allow her that privileged relationship. The women of Bethlehem offered Ruth the highest praise when they told Naomi that her daughter-in-law loved her and was worth more than seven sons (Ruth 4:15). To have been worth more than seven men must have been a source of great self-esteem, and Ruth had it all!

Hannah

ह्

Y ou might not perceive of Hannah as a woman of self-esteem, for she was lacking the one thing that every woman of her time wanted—children. But Hannah was a woman greatly loved by her husband. We know that she was one of two wives, and the other wife, Peninnah, had children. This fact alone might have robbed Hannah of her sense of self-worth. However, Hannah was comforted by the knowledge that in spite of her barrenness, she was loved. She was even given a double portion of what her husband, Elkanah, gave to Peninnah and her children. The Bible very touchingly portrays this with the words, "but to Hannah he gave a double portion, because he loved her, though the LORD had closed her womb" (1 Samuel 1:5).

Even though Peninnah had children and was well provided for by her husband, she was jealous of the barren Hannah. It appears that Elkanah was a man who could afford to have a wife to love and a wife to bear children. Perhaps Peninnah would have preferred to have been the one who was greatly loved, for love is a builder of self-esteem. Peninnah's self-esteem had to be pretty low, for she provoked and irritated Hannah and constantly reminded her that she was childless. People of low self-esteem frequently try to reduce others to their own low levels, and Peninnah was no exception. Hannah was obviously hurt, for she would not eat and was reduced to tears. *Have you ever felt unloved? Have you ever felt unlovable? Do you ever remind yourself how much God loves you?*

Elkanah asked, "Hannah, why do you weep? Why do you not eat? Why is your heart sad? Am I not more to you than ten sons?" (1 Samuel 1:8). Although Elkanah was asking these questions in an attempt to comfort, it is clear that he knew what had caused her distress. Hannah was comforted by her husband's expression of love, and her self-esteem was revived to the point that she decided to take her case to God in prayer.

Peninnah had challenged her sense of worth as a person; yet, Hannah knew that she was worthy. She entered into fervent prayer asking God specifically for a male child and making sacred promises in exchange for this blessing. We know that Hannah's self-esteem was restored, for she confronted Eli, the priest, who, seeing her lips move without uttering a sound, believed her to be drunk. She assured Eli that she was not drunk but had been engaged in fervent, silent prayer. She said, "Do not regard your servant as a worthless woman, for I have been speaking out of my great anxiety and vexation all this time" (1 Samuel 1:16). Hannah knew that she was not worthless, and she wanted Eli to know it also. She even left with Eli's blessing and wish for God's granting of her requests. This self-assured woman had not only convinced the priest that she was not drunk, but she had also earned his assistance in joining her in prayer. She must have left Eli feeling confident that God would grant her request.

Surely Hannah was a woman of self-esteem. Just look at the promises she made in exchange for a child. She promised to give the child to God for life, and this child would be her first born. Hannah may have remembered something about the first fruits, and perhaps in giving the first she would be blessed with others. Hannah must have believed herself to be special; her sense of self-esteem was well intact. I think she believed that any child of hers would be worthy of a lifetime commitment to God and would be used as a special messenger for God. Hannah was even bold enough to promise that her son would be alcohol free and his hair would never be cut. (Uncut hair was a visible symbol of consecration to God's service.) With her prayer and her promise,

Hannah exceeded the three barren biblical women, Sarah, Rebekah, and Rachel, who preceded her. All had grieved because of their barrenness, yet Hannah was the only one who engaged in fervent prayer and made a solemn vow of expectation for the life of her child. I wonder how many women today would be willing to make a vow of dedication and commitment to God for their child.

Not only was Hannah willing to engage in fervent prayer alone, but by soliciting Eli's assistance she was a living testimony to the words of the New Testament that would be written many years later, "Therefore confess your sins to one another, and pray for one another, so that you may be healed. The prayer of the righteous is powerful and effective" (James 5:16). To these words Hannah could say, "Amen!"

After Eli had joined her in prayer, Hannah left convinced that her prayers would be answered. She joined her husband, ate and drank, and was no longer sad. She expected her miracle as would any woman of self-esteem. She returned to the temple the next morning, worshiped God, and continued in prayer and thanksgiving believing that God had already answered her prayers. And God remembered Hannah. She bore a son whom she named Samuel, for she said, "I have asked him of the LORD" (1 Samuel 1:20b). Hannah's sense of self-worth was complete, and Peninnah, in a manner befitting an agent of provocation and ridicule, was not mentioned again.

Abigail

ও

Some might call her the woman who married the wrong man, but it was while she was in that bad marriage that she discovered herself to be a woman of tremendous self-esteem. Being forced to the forefront, she was able to help one of God's most powerful servants discover his mission and ministry. Her name was Abigail and she was married to Nabal, a very rich and very foolish property owner who lived in Carmel. According to the scripture, Abigail was "clever and beautiful," but her husband was "surly and mean" (1 Samuel 25:3*b*). The powerful man of God with whom she interacted was David.

The encounter in which the three became involved occurred after the death of the prophet Samuel. (Remember that Samuel was the much prayed for son of Hannah, and he became the faithful servant of God who anointed David as future king over Israel.) After mourning for Samuel and seeking to hide from Saul, David and six hundred of his men went into the wilderness near Carmel. The men protected and provided for Nabal's shepherds while they protected David from Saul. It was the time for shearing sheep, and as the day of great feasting approached, David sent his men to greet Nabal, inform him of the protection they had provided, and ask for food. But Nabal insulted them and sent them away empty. David was greatly offended by this rebuff, and instructed his men to strap on their swords. He intended to seek revenge.

But one of Nabal's servants explained the situation to Abigail, and even commented that misfortune would come to all of them because of Nabal's evil nature. Having worked in the household of the woman described as "clever and beautiful," the servant must have felt confident that armed with the facts, Abigail would make the right decision. Even though she had previously remained in the background, he knew her to be a strong woman who had the power to respond. She was a woman of self-esteem, and she would not let others suffer if she could help it. And she could. She was a wise peacemaker, a woman of great vision.

Abigail knew immediately what to do. She loaded donkeys with an abundance of food, purposely did not tell her husband, and followed her servants to meet David as he was approaching to do battle. David had just been recounting his acts of kindness in protecting Nabal's shepherds and vowed not to leave "so much as one male of all who belong to him" (1 Samuel 25:22b). But upon seeing him, Abigail fell at his feet and begged him not to take seriously such a foolish man as Nabal. She warned David to remain free of blood, guilt, and vengeance.

Abigail begged for forgiveness and asked that all blame and guilt be placed on her. She offered her gifts of delicious food, and she informed David of his mission. She told him that the Lord would bless his reign and those in his house because he was fighting God's battles. She said that evil would not be found in him all the days of his life and that while his life would be protected in the arms of God his enemies would perish. She ended her speech by saying, "When the LORD has done to my lord according to all the good that he has spoken concerning you, and has appointed you prince over Israel, my lord shall have no cause of grief, or pangs of conscience, for having shed blood without cause or for having saved himself. And when the LORD has dealt well with my lord, then remember your servant" (1 Samuel 25:30-31).

Abigail had a clear vision of David's ministry, and she did not want him to dirty his hands with the blood of a fool like her husband Nabal. I am sure that Abigail had seen many foolish men, but very few true servants of God. She did not want her family in any way to be responsible for the guilt that the new king of Israel might bear. But, at the same time, Abigail probably knew that her future with the evil and foolish Nabal was not secure, and she astutely asked David to remember her when the kingdom became his.

Consider the implications of all that Abigail did. Knowing that her husband was a foolish drunkard, she took matters into her own hands. She did not wait for the results of the insults her husband had hurled. She cared, protected, and sought to save her household. She carefully ordered the preparation of delicious food. *Does this detail call to mind any incident in your life when such a distraction seemed precisely the right thing to do? What is the relation of such an incident to self-esteem?* Then she greeted David as though he were already the king. She bowed before him and foretold his future and even solicited his remembrance. She was indeed a skillful woman of self-esteem.

And David listened to the beautiful and clever Abigail. He blessed God for her; he blessed her good sense; and he blessed her. David saw her confidence, her wisdom, and her poise. He accepted her gifts and returned her to her house in peace. Abigail had a calming effect on David. She had assured him about who he was, whose he was, and what he was to become. She had kept him free from the sin of revenge. Abigail returned to her home confident that her mission had been accomplished.

For the second time in one day, Abigail kept something from her husband. She had not told him that she was going to David, and when she returned, she did not tell him where she had been. She found him drunk and did not waste her time trying to explain what had happened. But the next morning when he had sobered, she did tell him about David and her journey. The news so stunned him that he was disheartened. He probably knew that he looked like a fool to David and his men, for his wife had defied his actions and offered food to them. He also finally knew for certain that these men really did represent the man who would be king and that he would never again be respected. Nabal was heartsick, and ten days later he was dead.

And again, Abigail's wisdom shines through. Just as she had predicted to David, God had taken care of his enemies. David did not need to dirty his hands; Nabal's own foolishness had killed him. Abigail was left rich and available.

When David learned of Nabal's death, he was grateful to God that Nabal had been punished for his own wickedness and that he (David) had not had a hand in it. He remembered Abigail, even as she had requested in her plea, and he sent for her to join him as his wife. David had recognized her goodness, her beauty, her wisdom, and he had praised her coming into his life. He knew that she was the kind of wife that he needed as he assumed the throne. Abigail was blessed of God, and the servant whom she informed of his mission invited her to join him. Yes, Abigail qualifies; she was a woman of great self-esteem!

The Woman
of Abel

૨●

*T*he woman of Abel is identified only as a "wise woman"
(2 Samuel 20:16), and as a woman of self-esteem she certainly
lives up to that description. Her town of Abel was being attacked
by David's commander, Joab, because it was harboring Sheba,
David's enemy. She could not stand idly by while the walls
surrounding the town were being knocked down and its people
massacred. Knowing what had to be done and being confident
that she was able to do it, she boldly took charge.

The wise woman of Abel cried out to Joab, pleading with him
to listen to her. When she had made sure that she was talking to
the right person, she stated her credentials. She said, "They used
to say in the old days, 'Let them inquire at Abel'; and so they
would settle a matter. I am one of those who are peaceable and
faithful in Israel; you seek to destroy a city that is a mother in
Israel; why will you swallow up the heritage of the LORD?"
(2 Samuel 20:18-19). This woman was not just anyone; she was
a peaceful, faithful mother. There was no reason that Joab or his
king would or should want to kill her or the town that had a
history of being a seat of wisdom.

Her words got Joab's attention, and he responded, "Far be it
from me, far be it, that I should swallow up or destroy! That is
not the case! But a man of the hill country of Ephraim, called
Sheba son of Bichri, has lifted up his hand against King David;

give him up alone, and I will withdraw from the city" (2 Samuel 20:20-21). Without a moment's hesitation, the woman of Abel promised to deliver Sheba's head. She believed in her ability to convince the townspeople to sacrifice the outsider who hid in their midst for the good of the whole town. She knew they trusted in her wisdom, and she felt the need to save the town that was a part of the "heritage of the LORD" (2 Samuel 20:19b).

And convince her people she did. They threw the head of Sheba to Joab who promptly disbursed his troops and returned to the king. The woman of Abel had found a need and filled it. She had used her wisdom to save her town. She had taken bold action. She was a woman of self-esteem! *Think about a time when you have quickly and boldly taken action. Where did you find your strength? What was the effect on your feelings of self-worth?*

The Widow of Zarephath

❧

*T*he widow of Zarephath, like so many other women, was never even named in the Bible, but she was indeed a woman of self-esteem. Although poor in possessions, she was rich in spirit and had been identified by God as one to whom his prophet Elijah should turn for help. Her story is told in 1 Kings 17:8-24, and its importance is underscored when Jesus recalls it in Luke 4:25-26, mentioning that there were many widows in Israel in the time of Elijah, "yet Elijah was sent to none of them except to a widow at Zarephath in Sidon" (Luke 4:26).

God instructed Elijah to, "Go now to Zarephath, which belongs to Sidon, and live there; for I have commanded a widow there to feed you" (1 Kings 17:9). The widow had already been commanded by God, so it is obvious that she knew and was known by God. This is the first clue that we have to her sense of self-esteem. Women of self-esteem know God and realize that they, in turn, are known by God. When Elijah met the widow as he entered the town, he noticed that she was gathering sticks and called out to her to bring him some water. Even though there had been an extensive drought and famine, the widow quickly responded to his request for water. Realizing that she was obeying the command already received from God, Elijah tested her further by asking for a morsel of bread. This was the point at which the widow's faith was sorely tried. She knew that God had commanded her to obey, yet she began to wonder if this was really the man of God she was expecting. So she presented her case by saying, "As the LORD your God lives, I have nothing baked, only a handful of meal in a jar, and a little oil in a jug; I am now gathering a couple of sticks, so that I may go home and prepare it for myself and my son, that we may eat it, and die" (1 Kings 17:12).

This woman of self-esteem was seeking to protect herself and her son. She had to be certain of Elijah's intentions. Would he simply command her to do as he had said or would he in some way assure her of his knowledge of the God whom she had promised always to obey? *How do you make decisions when you are unsure of God's will? Do you ever find it difficutl to trust persons who do not share your faith?* Elijah's response put the widow's mind at ease. He said to her, "Do not be afraid; go and do as you have said; but first make me a little cake of it and bring it to me, and afterwards make something for yourself and your son. For thus says the LORD the God of Israel: The jar of meal will not be emptied and the jug of oil will not fail until the day that the LORD sends rain on the earth" (1 Kings 17:13-14).

These words assured the widow that Elijah knew the God she served, for she was well familiar with the practice of giving of the first fruits to God. In the history of the faithful, those who had given first to God had always had enough, and Elijah had promised that she would never run out. She was willing to obey the command and give to God first through the prophet, having the faith that she and her son would not have to prepare to die. Elijah was able to speak to the widow in full confidence of God's promise to supply her needs, for he had just been delivered from the wrath of the evil Jezebel. He knew something about God's power to supply all our needs, and his confident manner in approaching the widow gained her confidence too. She believed him and she believed the God he served.

This widow of self-esteem found God's word to be true, and neither her meal nor her oil was ever depleted. But the true test of her faith and commitment was yet to come. Her son became ill, and she began to wonder why God had spared him from starvation. She even began to wonder what sins she had committed that might have resulted in the illness and eventual death of her son. She approached Elijah saying, "What have you against me, O man of God? You have come to me to bring my sin to remembrance, and to cause the death of my son!" (1 Kings 17:18). Elijah did not answer her question, he simply tested her faith. He said, "Give me your son" (1 Kings 17: 19). Would this widow who had obeyed all that God had commanded trust Elijah with the body of her dead son? Did she think enough of herself to believe that the good God that she served could not possibly take her son as atonement for her past sins? Could this man of God restore her son to her as he through God had replenished the meal and the oil? *What is the difference between self-esteem and faith?* She had obeyed him before and she would obey him again. Deep down she believed that he could help her or she never would have approached him in the first place. Her son was dead; why didn't she just bury him and not trouble Elijah any further? After all, he had done all that he could do by providing them with food. But she, like so many other women of self-esteem, just could not quit. She had to ask, "Why?"

Obeying Elijah one more time, this widow presented the son whom she held at her bosom and hoped that somehow Elijah would ask God to bring him back to life. And that is exactly what Elijah did. In dramatic fashion Elijah pleaded with God to restore the boy's life, and after stretching out upon him three times, the boy was revived. This test of faith for both the widow and Elijah became a vehicle for the demonstration of God's healing power. When Elijah presented the living child to its mother, she was convinced without a doubt that Elijah represented the God she served. She said, "Now I know that you are a man of God, and that the word of the LORD in your mouth is truth" (1 Kings 17:24).

This widow of self-esteem had learned that God is not limited either in providing food or in restoring life. She learned that

God's omnipotence and power is revealed in accordance with our faith. As she was faithful, so was God generous in revelation. The widow had learned that God is revealed to people of faith, and this revelation enhances their sense of self-worth. Hers was a lesson that all women of self-esteem must learn.

The Widow with Inexhaustible Oil

❧

*A*lthough she was a poor widow with two children living in a time of economic distress, she was acquainted with the prophets. Perhaps her husband had even been one of them, and she appealed to Elisha for help. When she approached him, she even claimed that he knew her husband to be a God-fearing man (2 Kings 4:1). When Elisha responded to her plea, her opportunity to prove herself to be a woman of self-esteem emerged.

The widow found herself burdened with the debts of her husband. His creditors showed her no mercy and demanded payment. All the woman had was her sons, and the creditors were threatening to take them as slaves in payment of the debts. *Can you imagine how this poor woman must have felt?* All she had of value was her sons and the creditors were about to take them. *Could you bear to stand by and allow your sons to be taken as slaves?* Well, no woman of self-esteem would, and this widow was not about to. Because she believed in her own worth, she also believed in that of her sons. Surely God had greater plans for their future than slavery could provide.

Elisha could not ignore her plea. He appreciated the life her husband had led, and he knew that this widow would continuously petition him if he did not find a way to help her. So, he asked, "What do you have in the house?" (2 Kings 4:2a). He knew that God would show him a way to help her use whatever she had to save herself and her children from the fate that awaited. The God the prophet and the widow served was like that. They knew that God could take whatever was offered in faith and use it, no matter how meager it might be, to cause a miracle. Elisha knew it, and this widow of self-esteem had to believe it or she would never have approached him in the first place.

The widow looked about her house and wondered what she had besides her sons. The answer was obvious because she had so little. Her response was, "Your servant has nothing in the house, except a jar of oil" (2 Kings 4:2b). Elisha did not question her response for he immediately saw God's solution to her dilemma. He gave her these specific instructions, "Go outside, borrow vessels from all your neighbors, empty vessels and not just a few. Then go in, and shut the door behind you and your children, and start pouring into all these vessels; when each is full, set it aside" (2 Kings 4:3-4). This woman of self-esteem did not question Elisha's instructions. She listened to all that he instructed, for she was confident that he was directing her in the way that God had revealed to him. She recognized that her responsibility was to be willing to follow in faith.

Like other self-assured women, this widow was in full control of her household. She told her children what they were to do to help solve the predicament in which they found themselves, and as the obedient sons she had raised, they responded. Without questioning her instruction, they started appealing to the neighbors for vessels and returned to their mother with them. From her one vessel of oil she was able to fill as many vessels as her sons were able to bring, and according to Elisha's instructions, they brought more than a few. Her supply of oil was inexhaustible. "When the vessels were full, she said to her son, 'Bring me another vessel.' But he said to her, 'There are no more.'

Then the oil stopped flowing" (2 Kings 4:6). The oil did not stop flowing until all the vessels were full, and the widow did not stop pouring until there were no more vessels. Women of self-esteem keeping pouring in faith, knowing that the supply of God's blessings will not run out. As the acts of faith keep going out to God, the blessings keep pouring in.

As soon as the widow had done all that Elisha had instructed, she returned to him for further instruction. We might wonder why she did not immediately start to sell the oil or use it to relieve her predicament. As a woman of self-esteem, she might have proceeded as she thought best. But this woman was wise enough to know that she had not even conceived of the oil as a vehicle to help solve her problems, so she was wise enough to return to the one who had advised her in the first place. Some women of self-esteem, like Eve, err because they are not obedient to the source from which their help comes. They are overly confident; they do not listen; they do not meditate and wait for the Lord. But, this widow was not like that. She had sought help from the man of God, and she knew that she must act only at his direction. Elisha said, "Go sell the oil and pay your debts, and you and your children can live on the rest" (2 Kings 4:7). Thus having received the okay from the man of God, the widow was able to clear her debts and save her sons from slavery.

Women of self-esteem know where their resources are. This widow knew that Elisha, her oil, and her sons were her resources. She also knew how to use each one of them. Like other women of self-esteem, she was in touch with a God whose servants could assist her in her hour of need. She was neither ashamed nor too proud to ask for assistance, and she was willing to take and follow instructions. Her rich reward and blessing was the freedom of her sons and a source of support for the rest of her life. Women of self-esteem become living witnesses to God's miraculous power.

The Shunammite Woman

꙳

*T*he Shunammite woman is one of the wealthy women of self-esteem appearing in the Scriptures. She had a comfortable home, a husband, and everything a woman could want except the one thing that so many women of that time wanted—a child. Yet, because she was a woman of self-esteem, she knew that even barren she was worthy and had learned to accept her circumstances. She knew and loved God and wanted to serve God in any way that she could.

She had heard of the man of God, Elisha, who had succeeded Elijah as the prophet of the area. Her house was well equipped and made a wonderful place for travelers to stop, so she invited Elisha to share a meal with her whenever he was in her area. Elisha loved the welcome and the wonderful food he enjoyed whenever he stopped there.

Noting the joy that Elisha's visits brought to her and to the prophet himself, the Shunammite woman said to her husband, "Look, I am sure that this man who regularly passes our way is a holy man of God. Let us make a small roof chamber with walls, and put there for him a bed, a table, a chair, and a lamp, so that he can stay there whenever he comes to us. (2 Kings 4:9-10). Because she was a strong, confident, self-assured woman, her husband agreed to her request, and the room was made.

Elisha was thrilled with the kind gesture and wanted to somehow reward her thoughtfulness, so he sent his servant,

Gehazi, to ask if there was anything he could do to repay her. Being the kind of woman that she was and living among her own people, she did not need any special favors from the king or from anyone else. She was happy just to have been able to serve the man of God. But Gehazi commented, "Well, she has no son, and her husband is old" (2 Kings 4:14b). Just what was Gehazi saying? Was he reminding Elisha that the one thing this woman did not have was what every woman wanted? Was he also letting him know that if her dream was ever to be realized, it had better be soon? Elisha did not bother to quiz Gehazi, he simply said to him, "Call her" (2 Kings 4:15a).

As the Shunammite woman entered the room, Elisha informed her that in due time she would hold her own son. We can only imagine her shock at this news. After being married for so many years and having a husband who was advanced in age, how could this man of God promise such a thing? Her only response was, "No, my lord, O man of God; do not deceive your servant" (2 Kings 4:16b). Although she wanted to believe him because he was a man of God and because she had prayed so long for a son, she did not want to be tricked into expecting a miracle that would never be realized. *How is self-esteem tied to hope? Have you ever been afraid to hope? Why?*

If Elisha replied to her plea, it is not recorded. In fact, no record is given of the woman's discussing the words and the promise of the man of God with her husband. The Scriptures just skip to the fact of the fulfillment of the promise. The woman bore a son in due time, within the year. She did not have to wait for her miracle any longer than the time it normally takes to bear a child. She knew almost immediately that the prophet was not deceiving her.

The Shunammite woman's joy must have been complete. She finally had everything she wanted. She had been truly blessed, and all because she had sought to make a visitor comfortable in her home. God was certainly a good God, worthy of praise.

But as all women of self-esteem discover, often there are tears interspersed with joy in life. She would have to learn to count it all joy. Accordingly, one day her much loved child complained to his father of a headache and was taken to his mother. She held him on her lap until life had passed from him. Being the strong woman that she was, she refused to accept the fact that the child was dead. She placed him on the bed in the room of the man of God, and she asked for a servant and a donkey so that she could quickly journey to the place where Elisha was. Her husband, not knowing that the child was dead, asked her why she wanted to go to Elisha. Not actually answering his question, she simply replied, "It will be all right" (2 Kings 4:23b). What a wonderful and positive thing to say! It is the true response of a woman of self-esteem. Such a woman is always hopeful and always full of faith. The God she served who was able to grant a barren woman a child was also able to restore a dead child, and she knew it. No matter what happened, it would be all right!

When the Shunammite woman reached Elisha at Mount Carmel, he knew that something was wrong, but the Lord had not revealed it to him. He sent Gehazi to meet her and told him to ask if everyone in her house was all right. This time she answered, "It is all right" (2 Kings 4:26b). The woman had reached her destination, and as soon as Elisha was in view, it was all right. She grabbed Elisha and said, "Did I ask my lord for a son? Did I not say, Do not mislead me?" (2 Kings 4:28). This distressed woman wanted to remind Elisha that she had been content as she was. Why had he fulfilled her dreams only to leave her empty again? She had not missed holding a baby in her arms because she had never held one, but once she had, she knew that life would never be the same. She had to make sure that Elisha got the message.

Elisha gave his staff to Gehazi and instructed him to place it on the child's face, but the Shunammite woman knew that the servant was not the man of God. Although this woman of self-esteem did not object to Gehazi's going to her child, she refused to leave without Elisha. Her child deserved the best and she intended to get it for him. Observing that she had no intentions of taking no for an answer, Elisha agreed to accompany her to the child. Having preceded them in reaching the child, Gehazi, as instructed, had laid Elisha's staff on his face with no results. It was left up to Elisha who quickly took matters into his own hands.

Elisha went to the room and closed the door on himself and the dead child. Then he humbly knelt in prayer. All he could do was to go to the source of all healing. He needed greater power than that contained in his staff. He needed God to intervene. God directed him to lie, full body on the child, "putting his mouth upon his mouth, his eyes upon his eyes, and his hands upon his hands; and while he lay bent over him, the flesh of the child became warm" (2 Kings 4:34). Elisha knew that God had heard his prayer. He was so full of the healing power of God that he had to get up and walk around the room before he could return to watch the child sneeze seven times before opening his eyes.

Elisha sent for the Shunammite woman and presented her child to her. Before taking hold of the child who had been restored to life, she fell at Elisha's feet in praise and thanksgiving. Women of self-esteem who meditate and pray, as did this woman, never forget where their help comes from, and they are willing and anxious to express their thanks. They do not miss a day praising God's name.

The Shunammite woman offered freely to share her earthly blessings with the man of God, and she was rewarded beyond her imagination. She was cautious in accepting her reward, but then she was steadfast and fierce in protecting it. She was faithful; she was confident; she was persistent; and she was rewarded. She was a woman of self-esteem!

Naaman's Maid

❧

She had been captured by Naaman, army commander for the king of Damascus, during a raid of the Israelite territory in which she lived. She served as a maid in his household, and she was normally quiet about her faith. But her master was ill, suffering from leprosy, and she knew that the God she served could heal him. Because she was a woman of self-esteem, faithful in meditation, prayer, and praise, God revealed a plan to her. In order for God's plan to be realized, she had to find a way to direct her master to the great prophet of her Lord.

She prayed about the action she should take, and after receiving the answer to her prayers, she boldly approached Naaman's wife and said, "If only my lord were with the prophet who is in Samaria! He would cure him of his leprosy" (2 Kings 5:3). Just imagine, a maid, a household servant, had confidently suggested a way to cure the master. No one had asked her opinion; no one even thought she had an opinion; but she knew that what she had spoken was the truth, for God had revealed it to her. Those brave words started a sequence of actions that led to one of Elisha's great miracles. The maid must have spoken her words with the strength and conviction of a woman of self-esteem, for she was believed without question, and the road that led to a cure was embarked upon.

First, Naaman's wife told her husband what the maid had said; then Naaman told his king, and then his king sent him to the king of Israel with a letter, money, and clothes requesting a cure.

Naaman's king was so sure that only Israel's king would have the power to cure that he did not mention the prophet whom the maid had intended. The request angered the king of Israel who tore his clothes and said, "Am I God, to give death or life, that this man sends word to me to cure a man of his leprosy? Just look and see how he is trying to pick a quarrel with me" (2 Kings 5:7). But Elisha heard about the request and sent this message to the king, "Why have you torn your clothes? Let him come to me, that he may learn that there is a prophet in Israel" (2 Kings 5:8).

The bold actions of a captured maid would serve as the vehicle to demonstrate that there was a prophet in Israel. *Have you ever been tempted to remain silent about something, but nagging feelings have remained with you? How have you overcome your initial inclination?* What if this young woman had remained silent? Would God have found another way to reveal that there was a prophet in Israel? Perhaps. But God had selected a woman of self-esteem who had enough faith and confidence in her own relationship with God that she dared to suggest that the God she served was able to cure all kinds of ills, even the dreaded leprosy. All her master needed to do was to go to God's prophet in Israel. After she had delivered her powerful message, she was confident that God would do the rest.

But it would not be easy because Naaman expected to be touched personally by God's prophet, Elisha. Elisha had simply sent word to Naaman to go wash seven times in the Jordan and he would be cured. Naaman could not understand how the Jordan could contain healing powers when the rivers of Damascus did not. He would have simply ignored the seemingly foolish advice of Elisha, but his servants approached him saying, "Father, if the prophet had commanded you to do something difficult, would you not have done it? How much more, when all he said to you was, 'Wash, and be clean'?" (2 Kings 5:13).

Naaman decided to follow the simple directions and was cured. He returned to Elisha proclaiming that the God of Israel was the only god in all the earth. The maid, God's young woman of self-esteem, had accomplished the crucial task; she had directed Naaman to Elisha; Elisha had with God's help cured Naaman; and Naaman had become a new witness for God. Thanks be to God for such a young woman of self-esteem!

Hulðah

*I*n the midst of idolatry Huldah remained steadfast in her worship of God and was able to redirect a nation. She was a prophetess, a woman of tremendous self-esteem. With her unique prophetic insight she correctly identified the book of the law found in the Temple to be the authentic word of God.

Judah as a nation had ceased to worship God. Idols had been built and even placed in the Temple dedicated to God alone. Forgotten was God's commandment, "You shall have no other gods before me"(Deuteronomy 5:7). But Judah had a good king, Josiah, one who loved God. His high priest, Hilkiah, found a book of the law in the Temple, and the words of that book were read to the king. Upon hearing those words, Josiah tore his clothes as a symbol of his great grief that his nation had strayed so far from the worship of God.

Josiah commanded Hilkiah and others of his officers, "Go, inquire of the LORD for me, for the people, and for all Judah, concerning the words of this book that has been found; for great is the wrath of the LORD that is kindled against us, because our ancestors did not obey the words of this book, to do according to all that is written concerning us" (2 Kings 22:13). In response to the command, "inquire of the LORD," the priest and the others went to the prophetess Huldah. Foremost as an authority of the Lord was Huldah, our woman of self-esteem. The text implies that it was believed that she could speak with authority for the Lord, for she had the Holy Spirit, meaning she was one to whom God's truth had been revealed. She could speak for God and King Josiah knew it.

Huldah was a married woman of great intellect and insight. She was highly respected because of her great love for God, and it was well known that God had spoken to her. She lived in Jerusalem in what was known as the Second Quarter, a place near the Temple, and it is significant that the king and the high priest did not send for her to come to them, but rather, they went to her. For them to go to her especially considering the time in which she lived, she must have been a very important woman, valued for her worth.

When Huldah was consulted, she responded without hesitation, "Thus says the LORD, the God of Israel" (2 Kings 22:15*a*). Huldah knew immediately that the book of the law (much of which is currently found in Deuteronomy) was authentic, and she could speak with authority. She kept repeating the phrase, "Thus says the LORD"; she wanted to make sure that they knew that it was the Lord and not Huldah who was speaking. She verified that all of the predictions of doom contained in the book would come true. Judah had indeed become an idolatrous nation, but King Josiah who loved the Lord and who had immediately expressed his remorse would be spared the impending disaster and would die in peace. He would not know the full wrath of God. He had been blessed with the spiritual insight to seek her advice and counsel. He had trusted her judgment and had sought to institute reforms.

Josiah knew that what Huldah had prophesied had come straight from God. He sought to cleanse the Temple of idols and encouraged the people to return to God. Josiah is remembered for the reforms he sought to bring about. *Recall a time when your action or advice had a wide-ranging effect. What did this incident do to your sense of self-esteem?*

Huldah did not hesitate as she spoke in response to the book of the law. She knew that she spoke for the Lord, and she spoke with power and authority. She was confident and self-assured. She was a woman of self-esteem and her prophecy helped to reform a nation.

Jehoshabeath

੶ஂ

*B*ecause Jehoshabeath was not afraid to do what she thought was right, I consider her to be a woman of self-esteem. Let us review the situation in which she found herself. Her father Jehoram did not walk in the ways of the great kings of Israel, and he was punished with a painful disease and death. His successor as king was her step-brother, Ahaziah, Jehoram's youngest son. King Ahaziah continued in the wicked ways of his father, for he was constantly coached by his evil mother, Athaliah. As the daughter of Jezebel, Athaliah was well trained in all that was evil, and she had spent her husband's reign keeping him on the wicked path.

After reigning only one year in Jerusalem, Ahaziah was killed, and his mother, Athaliah, seized the opportunity to assume the throne. In order to assure her unquestioned place on the throne, Athaliah "set about to destroy all the royal family of the house of Judah" (2 Chronicles 22:10*b*). This evil grandmother actually ordered the murder of all royal relatives, even her own grandchildren. But Jehoshabeath managed to rescue her nephew, Joash, one of the king's sons. She took him and his nurse to a bedroom and saved him from death at the hand of his grandmother.

Have you ever been asked to be so courageous? Why did Jehoshabeath dare to save even one child? She must have been God's instrument for preserving the reign of the house of David. Although the kings had strayed from the love of the Lord, there was still the possibility of restoration of the worship of God by the house of David if any of his descendants survived. If Jehoshabeath had not intervened, Athaliah would have succeeded in destroying all of David's royal family. God chose her to act. She was obedient; she did not fear her step-mother; she knew that she had to save at least one of her nephews; she did what she had to do; she did what she knew she could do; she did what God had revealed to her; and she did what was right. She was a woman of self-esteem.

Jehoshabeath managed to hide Joash long enough to escape with him to the temple where her husband, Jehoiada, was priest. They raised him for six years, and when the boy was seven they made his identity known, and he assumed the throne. Even though his evil grandmother, Athaliah, cried, "Treason! Treason!" (2 Chronicles 23:13b), she was killed with the sword.

As a result of Jehoshabeath's courageous act, a king of the line of David was again on the throne of Israel. Because of the king's young age, the priest, Jehoiada, did much in the way of restoring the worship of God and destroying the house of Baal. Joash was a good king as long as he had Jehoiada to guide him, but after Jehoiada's death, the king deserted the ways of the Lord.

When Jehoshabeath risked her own life to save her nephew and succeed in preserving through him the line of the house of David, she did not try to predict what kind of king Joash would become. She did not try to predict the future, for she knew that it was not her task to play God. She only wanted to act as God's instrument. She understood that God always makes a way. She and Joash were his way. She dared to respond; she risked doing what was right; she put her own life at risk; she was a woman of self-esteem.

Esther

ॐ

In your own life, what is the connection between self-esteem and success? Whenever we think of Esther, we ought to think of unlimited success. Esther was successful in all that she attempted, and of course, success is a great builder of self-esteem. But her success was not the source of her self-esteem; that came from within. Considering her heritage, we might have expected her to have grown up devoid of self-esteem, but that was not the case. Even though she was orphaned at an early age and was raised by her cousin, Mordecai, she had been steeped in the faith of the Jews. Mordecai may not even have wanted to raise her, but as a close male relative, she became his responsibility. As a man of great faith himself, he met his responsibility by imparting his faith to his young cousin. She had been raised to consider herself worthy.

Now Esther was a very beautiful young woman, and when Mordecai discovered that the king was in search of a beautiful young virgin to replace the queen who had been dethroned, he took Esther to the palace. As expected, Esther was one of the virgins selected for the twelve month beautification period in which oils and cosmetics were applied to enhance natural beauty. After the beautification period, Esther was chosen as the new queen. She was successful not only in being selected as one of the few to be beautified but also in becoming the final choice. Of course, her sense of self-esteem must have been at its zenith. But Esther's success was not to end with being crowned queen; she had a much greater role to play. She was to become the vehicle through whom all of her people would be saved.

There are certain characteristics that Esther possessed that figured prominently in her ability to succeed at the task God had for her. Each of these characteristics is indicative of her level of self-esteem. First, Esther was a listener, and successful people with self-esteem are willing to listen. She listened to Mordecai when he revealed the plot to kill the king. Her listening to Mordecai testified to the fact that once she became queen, she did not lose contact with her cousin. She was secure and self-confident enough to know that her status would not change if she associated with those outside the royal court. After all, she had been worthy when she had resided outside the royal court. So she accepted the information her cousin revealed, passed it on to the king, and the assassination plot was foiled.

Esther also listened when Mordecai came to her with the plan of Haman to kill all the Jews. She listened as he asked her to put her own life in jeopardy by going uninvited before the king to plead for the lives of her people. She listened as she was reminded that her being in the palace would not exempt her when all other Jews were killed. She listened when she was told that relief and deliverance for the Jews would come from another source if she did not help. And she listened when she was told, "Who knows? Perhaps you have come to royal dignity for just such a time as this" (Esther 4:14). Esther listened for she knew that in all that she heard, God was speaking to her and revealing her role in his plan.

Second, Esther was a learner. She learned from all that she heard. Some people listen but do not learn. The information made available to them just comes in one ear and goes out the other, but Esther was not like that. She acted on all that she heard. Being a woman of self-esteem, she knew that she was dependent upon others and others were dependent upon her. She knew where her success originated, and she knew that Mordecai was responsible for the success she had already attained by becoming queen. She did not forget all of those who had been left outside the palace walls. She had learned when she had been instructed in the faith, and she knew that Mordecai had been her primary instructor. Esther was a learner.

Third, Esther was a litigator. Being a woman of faith, she prayed, and then she acted, planned, and strategized. Preparing like any lawyer trying to win her case, she began her litigation. She agreed to go before the king even though she had not been called for thirty days. She knew that she would need to strategize carefully, for anyone who went into the king's inner court without having been summoned would be put to death. And she must have been painfully aware of the fact the former queen, Vashti, had been banished because she disobeyed the king by failing to appear when called for. Actually, Vashti must have had a measure of self-esteem herself, for she had refused to dance and parade before her husband and his drunken friends. She thought too much of herself to do that. So Esther would not be the first to violate the king's orders. Having all of this information before her, careful litigation was a must.

Esther knew exactly what to do. She asked all Jews to join with her in prayer and fasting. Esther knew that she would need the prayers of many to successfully survive the task ahead; and, how important it is for all of us to know, as did Esther, that we need the love, support, and prayers of others if we are to be successful. While her people were fasting and praying with her for success, Esther was formulating the rest of her plan. She knew that she would have to prepare the king for the request she was to make, and she knew that she needed to take her time in asking. Her strategy involved setting the mood by wearing the right clothes, serving delicious food, and inviting the people key to the judgment she desired before revealing her request. Consider how often business deals are closed in just such a manner. Yes, Esther was a great litigator.

Fourth, Esther was a lover of her people. She was willing to risk her life to save all Jews. Esther carefully selected her royal robes, sought to look her most beautiful, and went before the king knowing that she might perish. But the king was so taken with her beauty and regal appearance that he extended the golden scepter that signaled that she was not to be put to death even though she had appeared without invitation. "The king said to her, 'What is it, Queen Esther? What is your request? It shall be given you, even to the half of my kingdom'" (Esther 5:3). And with those words Esther put her carefully laid plans into motion. The end result was the death of Haman and the saving of the Jews. Again, Esther was successful and her sense of self-esteem demonstrated through her ability to listen, learn, litigate, and love is remembered to this day by all Jews as they celebrate the festival of Purim in her honor.

Judith

&❧

*J*udith was a heroine, a woman of great self-esteem who led the Jews to victory over the Assyrians. She may not be as familiar to you as are Deborah, Miriam, and Esther because the book that records her story is a part of the Apocrypha, those books outside the Jewish and Protestant canon. After having read the Apocrypha, it is hard for me to understand why these books were considered by Martin Luther and other Reformation leaders only to be "useful and good for reading" but not "equal to the Scripture."[4] There are many wonderful lessons in the Apocrypha, and of the several women who are highlighted, Judith is certainly worthy of mention as a woman of great insight, ability, confidence, and, yes, self-esteem.

Consider her situation. Judith is introduced in terms of her father, his ancestors, and her husband who belonged to her tribe and family. Nothing is said of any woman in the tribe and family, but Judith was paid the great honor of inheriting, after her husband's death, his gold, silver, slaves, livestock, fields, and estate. The Apocrypha records of her, "No one spoke ill of her, for she feared God with great devotion" (Judith 8:8). Her devotion to the customs and festivals of Judaism is noted in the fasting and prayer she offered as she mourned her husband's death. And yes, as we might expect, she "was beautiful in appearance, and was very lovely to behold" (Judith 8:7*a*).

4. Introduction to the Apocryphal/Deuterocanonical Books, *The Holy Bible New Revised Standard Version* (Nashville: Cokesbury, 1990).

Judith heard about the conquests of the powerful Assyrian army under the leadership of Holofernes, and she knew that the Israelites were ready to surrender. Their faith had failed, for they believed that God had already delivered them into the hands of the Assyrians because of their sins and the sins of their fathers. So the Israelites instructed their leader, Uzziah, to surrender. "But Uzziah said to them, 'Courage, my brothers and sisters! Let us hold out for five days more; by that time the LORD our God will turn his mercy to us again, for he will not forsake us utterly. But if these days pass by, and no help comes for us, I will do as you say'" (Judith 7:30-31). Uzziah actually believed that they could somehow force God to redeem them, for surely God would not forsake them forever.

But Judith set them straight. She sent her maid to summon them to her and then she told them, "Who are you to put God to the test today, and to set yourselves up in the place of God in human affairs? You are putting the LORD Almighty to the test, but you will never learn anything! You cannot plumb the depths of the human heart or understand the workings of the human mind; how do you expect to search out God, who made all these things, and find out his mind or comprehend his thought? No, my brothers, do not anger the LORD our God. For if he does not choose to help us within these five days, he has power to protect us within any time he pleases, or even to destroy us in the presence of our enemies. Do not try to bind the purposes of the LORD our God; for God is not like a human being, to be threatened, or like a mere mortal, to be won over by pleading" (Judith 8:12-16).

Judith was definitely a woman of self-esteem. She knew who she was and she knew who God was. She understood that God cannot be manipulated, that ultimatums do not work; and that God could deliver or destroy them. Judith was bold enough to tell this to her brothers, and she really did not care what they thought, for she was secure in her faith. She convinced the men around her that God was testing their faith and that the only proper reaction to this test was to give God thanks and praise. Uzziah responded to her reprimand by admitting that her wisdom was visible in her words and added, "Today is not the first time your wisdom has been shown, but from the beginning of your life all the people have recognized your understanding, for your heart's disposition is right" (Judith 8:29).

With these words, Uzziah asked for Judith's help, and she told him that she was about to do something that would go down through all generations of their descendants. Then Judith put into action the plan that God had revealed to her, and she asked that they not interfere with her. She was so confident that she even promised to abide by their five-day time limit. That is real self-esteem. She had faith in her ability to deliver; she knew that with God's help she would not fail.

Before Judith attempted to execute her plan she prayed. Her prayer was long and powerful. She gave God adoration and praise. She thanked God for leading her ancestor Simeon in revenge against Israel's oppressors, and she asked God to lead her, a widow. She called the Assyrians by name in her prayer and claimed that they knew neither God nor God's power and strength. She prayed, "For your strength does not depend on numbers, nor your might on the powerful. But you are the God of the lowly, helper of the oppressed, upholder of the weak, protector of the forsaken, savior of those without hope" (Judith 9:11). She pleaded with God to give her, a weak widow woman, the strength to strike down the oppressor of her people.

Once her prayer was completed, Judith got up to act. She was convinced that God was with her and that God would guide her in the successful fulfillment of her plan. Immediately she shed her mourning clothes, bathed, anointed herself with perfumed oils, put on her most festive attire and her fine jewelry, gathered food for the journey, and with her maid set about the destruction of the Assyrians. She knew who she was and what she had to do. She was a woman of great confidence.

When Uzziah and the Israelite leaders saw her, they were astonished by her beauty and wished her God's speed. Judith, professing to be a deserter, was captured by the Assyrians and taken to Holofernes on the pretense of providing him with a way to capture Israel without losing any of his men. Had Judith not been so beautiful and convincing as she began to unveil her plan, she might not have been taken to Holofernes but murdered or raped on the spot. However, the Assyrians "marveled at her beauty and admired the Israelites, judging them by her. They said to one another, 'Who can despise these people, who have women like this among them?'" (Judith 10:19a). Beauty does have its advantages and it certainly does not hurt in boosting one's self-esteem.

After Judith revealed what she wanted Holofernes to believe was her plan to assist him in the destruction of Israel, he and his servants said, "No other woman from one end of the earth to the other looks so beautiful or speaks so wisely!" (Judith 11:21). We can tell from this testimony that Judith had spoken with conviction. Judith refused the food offered from Holofernes' table, and ate what she and her maid had prepared. As a part of her overall plan, she also received permission to leave the camp each night to pray. She prayed for three nights, each time asking for the strength to carry out her plan of salvation for her people.

By the fourth day Holofernes was so enraptured by Judith that he could not resist the temptation to seduce her. He sent his servant to convince her to dine and drink with him so that he could satisfy his great longing for her. He even said, "it would be a disgrace if we let such a woman go without having intercourse with her. If we do not seduce her, she will laugh at us" (Judith 12:12). The role traditionally expected of beautiful biblical women is never more evident than it is here. Surely the very lusting after this woman gave her the opportunity to execute her plan for salvation. She would, because of his desire to seduce her, have complete and private access to the drunken enemy leader. How many women, both in modern and biblical times, have found themselves in this very same position? Remember Samson and Delilah; it was only because of their intimate bonding that Delilah had the opportunity to learn that shaving his head would remove his source of strength.

Judith beheaded the dead drunk Holofernes in his bed with his own sword and placed that head in her maid's food bag. Then according to her custom of three nights, she and her maid left the camp unhindered to pray. They returned to their own people and showed them the head of their enemy struck down by a woman who had escaped unharmed and undefiled because of her beauty, faith, and confidence. Upon discovering the body of their leader, the Assyrians, attempting to flee in panic, were easily captured and relieved of their great riches.

Judith, like Deborah and Jael before her, executed a plan that included violence. Both she and Jael beheaded an enemy, but they saved their people. Although we may not always agree with their methods, they did act based on their interpretation of what God had revealed to them. They believed in their ability to carry out God's plan, and they responded in faith. Judith and Jael were women of self-esteem, for they did what they believed was right regardless of the violent act that was demanded of them.

Judith led the women in praise before God while the men followed, and she dedicated to God all the bounty taken from Holofernes. This woman of tremendous self-esteem was honored all the days of her life. *What is the relationship between violence and self-esteem? Remember the story of Jael? When is such violence justified?*

Susanna

$\delta\!\!\!\!\!\!\backsim$

Susanna is another very beautiful Apocryphal woman of self-esteem. The Apocrypha includes her story in the thirteenth chapter of the Greek version of the book of Daniel. Although Susanna's story is not included within the accepted canon, it is well worth telling.

At the very beginning of her story, it is recorded that she is "a very beautiful woman and one who feared the LORD" (Susanna 2b). Susanna had been trained in the law of Moses by her parents and she had married a very rich and righteous man. These credentials assure us that she was a woman of self-esteem. She had beauty both inside and out; she had loving and righteous parents; and she had married a rich and honorable man. Each of these attributes is a source of confidence and esteem.

In biblical as well as in modern times there were and are wicked judges, and two of them frequented the home of Susanna and her husband, Joakim. Of course these wicked judges noticed the beautiful Susanna as she strolled in the garden. Although they were each consumed with lust for her, neither would admit to the other of his desires. Yet, they continued to watch for her each day. Then, as now, sexual passion could cause one to forget the purpose of one's business. These men were on a mission of administering justice, but all they could think about was seducing the beautiful wife of their host.

One day they individually decided to act on their sexual desire. So, having pretended to leave Joakim's house, they ran into each other as they each secretly returned. Upon questioning each other, they confessed their lustful intent and agreed to arrange a time they could find Susanna alone. That time came when Susanna was preparing to bathe in the garden and told her maids, "Bring me olive oil and ointments, and shut the garden doors so that I can bathe" (Susanna 17). Susanna was unaware that the two judges were hiding in the garden.

As soon as Susanna was alone, the two men approached her and begged her to relieve their burning sexual desire. They told her that if she refused, her fate would be in their hands, for they would testify that she sent her maids away because she had a young man with her. The judges had caught Susanna in what appeared to be a no-win situation. She knew that she would be condemned no matter what she did.

But this is where her sense of self-esteem made itself evident. Susanna knew that the sexual sin confronting her would mean death, but she had to believe that she had the ability to dispute their testimony. Somehow the God in whom she believed would have mercy on her if she did not submit to this wrongful act. She said, "I choose not to do it; I will fall into your hands, rather than sin in the sight of the LORD" (Susanna 23).

The respected but wicked judges carried out their threat and testified against Susanna. They claimed that she entered the garden, dismissed her maids, and proceeded to have a sexual encounter with a young man who was hiding there. They further stated that they were not able to hold the young man because of his youth and strength, but they did detain Susanna. However, she had refused to identify the man. All during their deceitful testimony, the judges feasted their eyes on the beauty of the woman who had chosen death over a liaison with them. *Think of a time when you stood firmly on the truth, even when it would have been easier not to do so. How did that situation affect your self-esteem?*

Although Susanna's friends and family did not want to believe what was being said against her, the judges who were respected elders in the community could not be disputed. Susanna was condemned to death.

Susanna cried out to God, "O eternal God, you know what is secret and are aware of all things before they come to be; you know that these men have given false evidence against me. And now I am to die, though I have done none of the wicked things that they have charged against me!" (Susanna 42-43). God heard her prayer and moved in the spirit of a young lad named Daniel who shouted in her defense, "I want no part in shedding this woman's blood!" (Susanna 46).

Daniel's outburst caused quite a stir. Everyone present wanted to know why he would not participate in the condemnation of this guilty woman. Daniel was bold enough to label as fools all of those who were considering condemning a daughter of Israel without either conducting an examination or attempting to learn the facts. His statement speaks well for Susanna's reputation. She must have been a fine woman, a daughter of Israel that in essence is a daughter of the commandment, Bat Mitzvah, versed in the keeping of a Jewish home, and certainly one who would not be guilty of the sin that she was charged with. I think that just by looking at the beautiful Susanna, Daniel could see her sense of self-esteem.

Daniel ordered everyone back to court and told the elders assembled to separate the two accusing judges. Once separated, Daniel proceeded to examine them individually. First confronting the judge with his past sins and wickedness and then intimidating him by telling him that his sins had come home, he asked him under which tree he had seen the woman and her lover being intimate. The judge responded, "Under a mastic tree" (Susanna 54b). Daniel accepted this response and then proclaimed that the lie just told would cost the judge his head.

The second judge was called before Daniel, and again Daniel greeted the accuser with condemnation for his past sins. God had given Daniel the vision of this judge's having been beguiled by Susanna's beauty and motivated by lust. He even told the judge of his prior intimidation of the beautiful daughters of Israel who had only submitted to his advances out of fear. But Daniel let him know that this proud daughter of Judah, Susanna, would not be intimidated. She had too much self-respect, too much self-esteem. Then Daniel asked this judge under what tree he had caught the lovers, and the response was, "Under an evergreen oak" (Susanna 58b). Again Daniel was able to proclaim that the lie had cost the liar his head.

All of those who had assembled joined in praise of God who had saved Susanna, a faithful servant. The judges were convicted of bearing false witness, and they received the death sentence that they had intended to inflict upon the beautiful Susanna.

Susanna received the praise of her parents, her husband, and all her other relatives. They were not only proud that she had been faithful to her training and was not guilty of the sinful act that she had been accused of, but they were also proud that she had relied on her faith in God to save her life. Women of self-esteem, like the beautiful Susanna, are not afraid to trust in God.

The Canaanite Woman

ॐ

T he Canaanite woman believed that even the crumbs of Jesus' healing power would cure her daughter. She did not need the whole dinner that appeared to be reserved for Israel's lost sheep. As a woman of self-esteem, somehow she knew that when we have real faith, crumbs are enough.

The Canaanite woman was bold enough to approach Jesus shouting to him to have mercy on her. In a very uncharacteristic manner, Jesus did not answer her. Jesus gave her the opportunity to demonstrate her faith. The Scripture says, "But he did not answer her at all. And his disciples came and urged him, saying, 'Send her away, for she keeps shouting after us.' He answered, 'I was sent only to the lost sheep of the house of Israel'" (Matthew 15:23-24). How would this poor woman respond to so harsh a reply? Was she not worthy of the Master's healing power? Being a woman of self-esteem, she did not go quietly away.

She had come for her daughter. Her daughter was possessed by a demon, and this great man of God about whom she had heard so much had the power to speak the word that would heal her daughter. She would not be denied. Somehow she had to convince the Master to grant just a crumb of his healing power. As a woman of self-esteem, she believed that even a crumb would be enough.

Kneeling humbly before him, she said, "Lord, help me" (Matthew 15:25). How could Jesus refuse to help anyone who asked sincerely and who recognized him as Lord? He did not refuse her request, he simply reiterated his mission only to the house of Israel by responding, "It is not fair to take the children's food and throw it to the dogs" (Matthew 15:26). This harsh statement might have sent anyone else running in defeat, but not this woman of self-esteem. She looked him straight in the eye and said, "Yes, Lord, yet even the dogs eat the crumbs that fall from their masters' table" (Matthew 15:27).

The Canaanite woman was not asking to be treated as one of the children of the house of Israel. Perhaps she did not dare to consider herself deserving of the whole meal that they were privileged to eat. All she wanted were the crumbs. No one could deny her that. Surely she was worthy of the crumbs. She knew that a crumb from Jesus would be enough for the healing power that her daughter needed, and she intended to persist until her request was granted. She loved her child enough, was bold enough and self-assured enough, to believe that she would not be denied. *Would you have had the same kind of faith? Would you have simply hung your heads and walked away in defeat?* The Canaanite woman, being a woman of self-esteem, "hung in there" and was rewarded.

Greatly impressed by her demonstration of faith, Jesus answered her, "'Woman, great is your faith! Let it be done for you as you wish' And her daughter was healed instantly." (Matthew 15:28). The woman had persisted to the point of having her wish granted, and she neither had to wait nor perform any special ritual or duty. Her wish of healing was granted instantly. She was a woman of self-esteem, and she believed that her request deserved a positive response from the one she addressed as Lord. She was willing to use the crumbs; she did not need the whole dinner reserved for the children. She knew that crumbs were enough! Hallelujah!

Pilate's Wife

ॐ

*T*he only words the Bible records that are attributed to Pilate's wife are these, "Have nothing to do with that innocent man, for today I have suffered a great deal because of a dream about him" (Matthew 27:19). But those words are sufficient for us to get a clear picture of her. She had courage and conviction, for she was bold enough to send that message to her husband as he sat on the judgment seat. She knew how very important her message was, for she sent her message even after Pilate had left their chambers and was about to render his decision.

Pilate and his wife were in Jerusalem for the Feast of the Passover. While Pilate was involved in making political decisions, I believe his wife probably had time to circulate among the people and hear of the man called Jesus of Nazareth. I believe she had heard of his miracles, his loving ways, and his kindness to children. Her woman's intuition told her that he was a good man. She could only wonder why the people who had hailed him as king on Sunday were now demanding his life. Surely he was innocent.

Proof of his innocence had come to her in a dream. God had revealed to her that this man was indeed innocent; in fact, she was convinced that he was God's Son. She had to intercede. She had to do whatever she could to keep her husband from being blamed for the death of an innocent man. She had to protect her husband's reputation, and she had to save Jesus. She did what she could. She sent the message.

Pilate faced a real dilemma. He could have ignored the charge of blasphemy, for that was a religious charge and in his political position he did not have to deal with religious charges. But Jesus' accusers were too clever to give him that easy way out. They presented Pilate with three political charges that he could not ignore. "They charged Jesus first with being a revolutionary, second, with inciting the people not to pay their taxes, and third, with claiming to be a king."[5] As governor, Pilate had to deal with those political charges; yet, his wife's message troubled him. What if this man truly was innocent? What would happen to the political future Pilate had planned?

Pilate thought he saw a way out. He was actually more afraid of the crowd than of trusting his wife's intuition. So he offered the crowd a choice. They could spare one criminal. He gave them the choice of Jesus or Barabbas, hoping to please both the crowd and his wife. But the crowd chose Barabbas, a known thief. All Pilate could do was declare that he had found no fault in Jesus and try to wash his hands of the whole affair. Pilate could not wash away his participation in the crucifixion. His hands were stained with the blood of the Master.

Pilate's wife had done all that she could to save Jesus and to spare her husband the guilt he would always bear. God had revealed to her that Jesus was innocent, and she had acted on that revelation. But it was not to be. God had a greater plan. She had borne witness to the innocence of Jesus, and we can salute her as a woman who spoke boldly her conviction against all odds. She was indeed a woman of self-esteem. *Have you ever acted on a dream? What risks were involved in your action? Did the result affect your self-esteem?*

---

5. William Barclay, *The Gospel of Matthew, vol. 2* (Philadelphia: The Westminster Press, 1975), p. 357.

The Woman with the Issue of Blood

ॐ

I wish this woman's name had been mentioned, for she is indeed a woman of great self-esteem. She refused to accept her infirmity and persistently sought healing. I particularly like the way Mark tells her story (Mark 5:25-34). Mark sets the stage for her incomparable encounter with the Lord.

At the time of their meeting, Jesus had grown in fame and popularity and was constantly surrounded by crowds of people seeking his healing powers. When our woman of self-esteem caught up with him, he was on his way to attend to the daughter of Jarius, the president of one of the synagogues. I can just imagine what she had heard about Jesus, and she, propelled by her great faith and belief that she deserved to be healed—and perhaps by desperation too, had decided that Jesus alone had the power to restore her health. Mark explains that this woman had been suffering from hemorrhages for twelve years. She had spent all that she had on doctors who had not cured her. In fact, her condition had worsened. Although you or I might just give up if we had exhausted our resources on doctors and found no satisfactory cure, this woman of self-esteem knew that if she persisted, she would not be denied. That is what I call real confidence.

As she approached Jesus she probably reasoned with herself, "This man of God has the answer to my problem. What I have heard about him makes me realize that his power comes from above. I have been spending my money on those who have medical knowledge but no faith. If I can just get close enough to touch him, I know that I will be cured."

If she had thoughts like these, I would say she was a woman of great self-esteem. Remember that this woman, because of her bleeding, was considered unclean. People had shunned her for twelve years. Because of her infirmity she was not welcome in the temple to worship, but she had not ceased to have faith that God would somehow, somewhere effect a cure for her. She still knew that God was able. In Jesus she saw her answer.

As she pushed through the crowd, she reviewed the three words that motivated her. The first word was *desire*. This woman really wanted to be healed. Healing for her was not just a mystical dream. It was a present and active desire. She wanted healing so badly that she had invested all of her resources to obtain it. *Have you ever wanted anything badly enough to risk investing all of your resources?* That commitment alone is an act of great faith.

The second word that motivated her was *discipline*. This very faithful servant had been extremely disciplined over the past twelve years. She had gotten up every day, sought out a doctor, and returned home in worse shape than she was when she had left; yet, she continued to pray that God would give her just enough strength to do it all over again the next day. That is what I call real discipline, but real discipline is characteristic of women of self-esteem.

The third word that motivated this woman was *determination*. She was determined to be cured. She was determined to touch Jesus. She was propelled by faith to touch a strange man whom she did not have permission to touch. She was willing to break this custom, for she knew that healing resided in his body. She was determined to once again be permitted to enter the temple and worship her God. It was not important that she had no more money and was in worse health than before. In spite of everything she had the faith that she would be cured. She would not be denied. She was driven by determination.

Once she was immersed within the crowd, the woman perceived that it might not be possible to actually touch Jesus, but she would not be deterred. She extended her faith to included simply touching something that was touching him—his clothes. She said, "If I but touch his clothes, I will be made well" (Mark 5:28). And she was, for, not eventually, not after twelve more years, but immediately the hemorrhage stopped, and she was healed.

Imagine the feeling that flowed through her body. She felt the power of the God moving, touching, and healing. She knew that her faith had been rewarded. At the same time, Jesus knew that power had left him, a power great enough to effect a miraculous healing. Jesus knew that there had been an investment of himself in another. Somehow we never produce anything great without an investment of ourselves. If it happens too easily, it probably will not have a lasting impact. Jesus knew that the power that had been drawn from him would last a lifetime.

And so he was prompted to ask the disciples what seemed to be a ridiculous question. He asked, "Who touched my clothes?" (Mark 5:30b). The logical response of the disciples, "You see the crowd pressing in on you; how can you say, 'Who touched me?'" (Mark 5:31), emphasizes the fact that Jesus had only impassively participated in the healing. It happened because of the woman's great faith. She did it herself by believing that healing was possible with Jesus.

Although the woman feared approaching Jesus, she knew that she had to claim the healing that had taken place in her body. So she approached him in great humility, falling at his feet in grateful praise, revealing all that had happened to her. Jesus did what no one had done in a long time. He claimed her as part of the family of God, his own family. He called her "daughter" and he told her that her faith had made her well. He recognized the desire, discipline, and determination that had been a part of her life for the last twelve her years, and he told her to go in peace, cured forever from her trouble. Her faith, her confidence, her sense of great self-esteem had drawn from the Master enough power to last a lifetime. Praise be to God!

The Widow Who Gave All

❧

*T*he unnamed widow who gave all that she had proved that one does not have to be rich in worldly possessions to be a person of self-esteem. This widow collected her two small coins, grabbed her worn coat, and proudly entered the Court of the Women at the Temple in Jerusalem. What could she have been thinking to enter the court in her shabby attire? She was thinking of her great love for God and how richly God had blessed her. She did not have the wealth of the others who had gathered there, but that did not matter. As a woman of self-esteem, she knew that the God she served looked on her heart and not at either her outward appearance or her worldly possessions. She was worthy, and God would accept whatever she had to offer.

Did this poor widow know that the givers were being observed? Had she any way of knowing that the story of her sacrificial gift would be told for generations? Did she know that her poverty would outlast wealth? Had she any idea that she was in the presence of the Savior of humankind? None of these questions was important to her. Her only mission was to give to the Temple in support of God's work.

There were several offertory receptacles, thirteen in all, and they were for "contributions for the daily sacrifices and expenses of the Temple."[6] The Scripture does not identify the receptacle

6. William Barclay, *The Gospel of Mark* (Philadelphia: The Westminster Press, 1975), p. 302.

in which she placed her meager contribution: we know only that her two coins represented everything she had. She had faith enough to give it all. She had probably worked hard for her two coins, and she did not know where her next coin would come from; yet she did not think in terms of one coin for me and one for God. She gave it all to God. She understood personal sacrifice. She had an intimate knowledge of giving until it hurts. But she had self-esteem, and women of self-esteem can afford to give all. They believe enough in themselves to be confident of survival. They understand that giving all empties us out so that God can fill us up. This widow woman of self-esteem was confident that the God she served would make it possible for her to earn other coins. Although she did not have much, she was alive and well, and God had never failed her.

As the widow proudly walked toward the receptacle, she could not help but notice the large sums that the rich people were giving. The rich were giving of their leftovers, but she was giving of her necessities. How she wished that she had more; yet, she was comforted by the knowledge that God knew both her willing spirit and her meager possessions. So she held her head high and proudly dropped in all that she had. Jesus immediately noticed her devotion to his Father and sensing her great sacrifice, he said, "Truly I tell you, this poor widow has put in more than all those who are contributing to the treasury. For all of them have contributed out of their abundance; but she out of her poverty has put in everything she had, all she had to live on" (Mark 12:43-44).

A woman of self-esteem knows that she can afford to give generously because God will provide again. She knows that God does not provide once and then desert you. One who is insecure holds on to what she has, for she fears that it will never be replaced. If she does not keep the little she has, she will be left with nothing. But the woman of self-esteem rejoices in the opportunity to demonstrate her faith. She is confident that God will direct her to more than adequate provisions. She knows as did the Canaanite Woman that crumbs are enough when one has faith, so she can afford to be generous. She is convinced that the value of the gift is determined by the spirit and sacrifice associated with it. Like this widow, women of self-esteem know how to give until it hurts, until it involves a personal sacrifice. Their very lives are controlled by faith. *Think of some incidents from your own life when self-esteem and generosity have been connected.*

Elizabeth

❧

She was a descendant of Aaron, married to a priest, and she lived "blamelessly according to all the commandments and regulations of the Lord" (Luke 1:6). Her life of faithfulness to God had made her a woman of self-esteem, and she was richly rewarded by God when she was chosen to be the mother of John the Baptist.

Elizabeth was obviously a woman of some means. Her husband, Zechariah, was highly respected as a priest, and she had come from a family of priests. She had everything but a child, and she had been subject to ridicule because of it. In biblical times, the woman was always blamed when a couple was childless. She was even pitied by others who had many children. But Elizabeth knew that even without children she could be a blessing to her husband and to others as she demonstrated her faith. Although she did not expect it, when she learned of the great miracle that God was about to perform in her life, she accepted it in faith. Zechariah did not. He expressed disbelief when he was informed that his elderly wife would bear a child.

The child that was to be born to Zechariah and Elizabeth was to be no ordinary child. He was to be "great in the sight of the Lord," and even before his birth he was to be "filled with the Holy Spirit" (Luke 1:15). Zechariah could not believe what he was told, and he was struck speechless. Elizabeth accepted this great blessing and responsibility and used her months of preparation to counsel with her husband and to share with her cousin, Mary, who was to be the mother of another very special child.

Just imagine Elizabeth's relief! She could finally anticipate sharing with other mothers as they discussed the antics of their children. She would know the joy of holding a child at her breast. She could rejoice as he took his first steps and spoke his first words. She would no longer feel disgraced or forgotten by the Lord. The Lord she served all of her life had remembered her, even in her advanced years, and she was grateful.

Elizabeth needed time to prepare to assist God in bringing this special child into the world, so she secluded herself for five months. Somehow Elizabeth had learned to just be still until the will of God became clear to her. She must have spent hours in prayer and meditation as she waited for God's guidance, for she knew that the child she carried would be filled with the Holy Spirit. I think she wanted to be able to communicate with this child, spirit to spirit.

When Elizabeth's period of seclusion had ended, God was ready to work through her as an instrument of healing for the maiden that was chosen to bear the Messiah. Elizabeth had already faced ridicule and public scrutiny for her barrenness. So when Mary found herself unmarried and pregnant, it was her cousin Elizabeth that she turned to for advice. Mary knew Elizabeth to be a woman who loved God. She also knew that Elizabeth had faced public humilation. Mary wondered how she should face the ugly stares. But she was confident that Elizabeth would know how she could reach beyond those obstacles, and would share with her all that she knew. *Think of a time when your faith and self-esteem have helped you assist someone who needed help.*

As Mary approached her cousin who was in the sixth month of her pregnancy, Elizabeth felt the baby that she carried leap in her womb. Elizabeth's unborn child was filled with the Holy Spirit and joyously greeted Mary's unborn babe whose presence he felt. This was the first witness to the joy that fills those who are in the presence of the Lord. And John's mother, Elizabeth, felt the Lord's presence also, for she greeted her cousin with the words, "Blessed are you among women, and blessed is the fruit of your womb. And why has this happened to me, that the mother of my Lord comes to me?" (Luke 1:42-43). Elizabeth knew that Mary was the mother of her Lord. As a woman of faith, God had revealed it to her. She felt especially blessed to have been chosen to be in the presence of Mary, and she accepted this blessing with humility and joy.

The lives of these two pregnant women would forever be changed because of the presence of the Lord. Even before he was born, Jesus managed to change lives. Two women who might never have been moved to speeches before were suddenly speaking with power and authority. Elizabeth had become the spokesperson for the family because her husband had been rendered speechless. Mary was moved to speak some of the most beautiful words of the New Testament, for in the presence of Elizabeth she said, "My soul magnifies the Lord, and my spirit rejoices in God my Savior" (Luke 1:47). The speeches given by these two women are some of the longest and most moving attributed to women in the New Testament.

After Mary expressed all that she was feeling, she remained with her cousin until just before she gave birth. Elizabeth truly became that source of strength that Mary had needed. As a woman of self-esteem, Elizabeth was able to help Mary in her own struggle for self-esteem. Elizabeth had prepared herself through her five months of seclusion, and now she was able to help prepare Mary. By the time Mary returned home, she was ready to await the birth of the Savior of the world.

Elizabeth was also ready, and her time of waiting had ended. She delivered her son, and after the prescribed eight days, she and Zechariah took him to be circumcised and named. Although all who were present expected the child to be named for his father, Elizabeth clearly stated, "He is to be called John" (Luke 1:60). This woman of self-esteem did not back down when she was questioned. She knew what the name was to be, and while her husband was speechless, she was able to abide by God's wishes. The name, John, "is a shorter form of the name *Jehohanan*, which means *Jehovah's gift* or *God is gracious*. It was the name that God had ordered to be given to the child and it described the parents' gratitude for an unexpected joy."[7] John was indeed an appropriate name, and all who were present knew that this child would have a special mission. But even though Elizabeth had spoken the name with all of the confidence and certainty that was characteristic of her, those officiating needed to know what the father said about the name. Zechariah was given a writing tablet, and he wrote, "His name is John" (Luke 1:63). Finally with the ability to testify to the power of God, Zechariah's tongue was loosened, and he began to speak, praising God. Oh, how wonderful to have the first words one speaks after almost a year of silence to be words of praise! Zechariah had become a witness while Elizabeth had witnessed all along. Women of self-esteem are often called on to do just that—to be witnesses all along!

---

7. William Barclay, *The Gospel of Luke* (Philadelphia: The Westminster Press, 1975), p. 17.

Mary

ᡒ

*H*ers was a common name in the times in which she lived, but because of who she became that name is loved and revered by Christians the world over. She was a teenager from a relatively poor and ordinary family, but I think she had to have been a young woman of tremendous self-esteem or she would not have been selected to be the mother of our Lord. How could so young a woman endure the stigma of becoming pregnant with a child during her period of engagement? What would her fiance think? How would her parents accept what had happened to their daughter, the daughter they had believed to be a virgin? Could the words of the angel possibly be true? Would others believe that an angel had actually appeared to her? She would have to draw on every ounce of her self-confidence in order to face the ridicule that awaited her.

During the year-long period of engagement, couples in Mary's lifetime were considered to be married except that there was to be no physical consummation until after the marriage ceremony. In fact, if the fiance were to die during this period of betrothal, it would be said that the young woman was a widow. "In the law there occurs the strange-sounding phrase,'a virgin who is a widow.' "[8] Who would believe that this pregnant, betrothed woman was a virgin?

Mary had received the greeting of the angel. She had been called a "favored one," and she had been told that the Lord was

---

8.   William Barclay, *The Gospel of Luke* (Philadelphia: The Westminster Press, 1975), p. 12.

with her (Luke 1:28). Although she had been frightened by the greeting and message of the angel, she had to still the rapid beating of her heart and reflect on the message. She had been called a "favored one," and this label must have enhanced her feeling of self-worth, but what did the rest of the message mean? "And now, you will conceive in your womb and bear a son, and you will name him Jesus. He will be great, and will be called the Son of the Most High, and the Lord God will give to him the throne of his ancestor David. He will reign over the house of Jacob forever, and of his kingdom there will be no end" (Luke 1:31-33). How these words must have disturbed this young woman. A million thoughts must have entered her mind, but being concerned with her reputation had to be primary among them as her response to the angel's message was, "How can this be, since I am a virgin?" (Luke 1:34). Mary knew that she and her dear betrothed Joseph had kept the law. How could she have a child? The angel answered, "The Holy Spirit will come upon you, and the power of the Most High will overshadow you; therefore the child to be born will be holy; he will be called Son of God. And now, your relative Elizabeth in her old age has also conceived a son; and this is the sixth month for her who was said to be barren. For nothing will be impossible with God" (Luke 1:35-37). The last sentence said it all. Nothing will be impossible with God! If Mary had ever believed in God, she had to know the truth of that statement. The God of her ancestors who had long awaited the Messiah from the line of David, that same, great God was about to effect a miracle through her. The Messiah would be conceived within her womb. She was indeed blessed and favored among women. Even her cousin who had lived a godly and righteous life and had longed for a child was well into her pregnancy. How great God was! Her only response to this news was, "Here am I, the servant of the Lord; let it be with me according to your word" (Luke 1:38).

Typical of a woman of self-esteem, Mary accepts her role in God's great plan for salvation. She is God's chosen servant and as such she must do all that God has so vividly revealed to her through the angel. Other women of self-esteem only believed that what they did was the right thing as revealed to them by God, but Mary had been visited by an angel. There was no doubt about what she was to do; she was to become the mother of God's own Son.

God knew that this young woman, who had been so carefully selected, would need the support of another woman of self-esteem. Therefore, God allowed the angel to tell Mary about the unexpected pregnancy of her cousin Elizabeth, who was now in her sixth month. Mary journeyed to visit Elizabeth whom she knew to be just the kind of mentor she needed. Interestingly enough, Elizabeth greeted Mary in the same way that the angel had. "Blessed are you among women" (Luke 1:42). Hearing herself called blessed and favored for the second time in a relatively short period of time did for Mary what it would have done for any of us. It enhanced her sense of self-esteem. She was really believing that she was a blessed and favored woman, and the wonderful words that came in recognition of her status are some of the most beautiful and revolutionary in the New Testament. These words are in fact some of the only ones in which there is a full speech dialogue involving a woman. "The Magnificat is the great New Testament song of liberation—personal and social, moral and economic—a revolutionary document of intense conflict and victory." [9] Mary was able to magnify and praise God who had not held her low estate against her, but had used a person of her status as the vehicle through which the Messiah should come into the world. She could proclaim the mercy of God to and for all who feared God, and she could foretell doom for the proud and vain. She could proudly recall the promise made to her Jewish people, and she knew that future generations would call her blessed—even as the angel and Elizabeth had. She knew herself to be a woman of self-esteem.

---

9. Jane Schaberg, "Luke," *The Women's Bible Commentary* (Louisville: Westminster/John Knox Press, 1992), p. 284.

Mary spent three months with her cousin and was comforted by the wisdom Elizabeth shared with her. Armed with new-found strength to face the ridicule that awaited her, Mary returned home to await her own first born. God had also prepared Joseph through the visit of an angel who told him to receive this child that Mary carried, and together they traveled to Bethlehem where God's Son was born. Mary realized the truth of the angel's proclamation that her child would be great, the Son of the Most High, for when the shepherds and the angels heralded his birth, she treasured and pondered their words in her heart (Luke 2:19).

Once the child was born, Mary had to keep the customs of the Jewish faith. She and Joseph had been given the child's name by the angel, and after eight days, he was circumcised and named Jesus. After the forty day period of purification, Mary was permitted to enter the Temple, and she and Joseph were able to present Jesus as holy to the Lord, offering the sacrifice stated in the law of Moses, "a pair of turtle doves or two young pigeons" (Luke 2:23-24). At this time Jesus was recognized both by Simeon and Anna as the source of salvation, the long-awaited light to the Gentiles.

This mother was well on her way to fulfilling her role in the salvation of us all. She taught and nurtured the child as he "grew and became strong, filled with wisdom; and the favor of God was upon him" (Luke 2:40). We are aware that she saw to his training and observance of the Jewish holidays, for each year her family traveled to the Temple in Jerusalem to observe Passover. It was when Jesus was twelve that he claimed his special kinship to God. When they discovered that he was missing from the group that was returning to Nazareth from the Passover festival, Mary and Joseph searched for the boy. Finding him in the Temple, he could not understand their distress. He said, "Why were you searching for me? Did you not know that I must be in my Father's house?" (Luke 2:49). Again, Mary "treasured all these things in her heart" (Luke 2:51). Mary knew that his mission, the reason for his extraordinary birth was being revealed to him. Her job was clear;

she was to help him increase "in wisdom and in years, and in divine and human favor" (Luke 2:52).

Mary obviously did her job well, for when Jesus started his ministry, she was not only present but instructional when his first miracle was performed. It was at the wedding in Cana of Galilee. After telling her son, "They have no wine," and ignoring his reply, "Woman, what concern is that to you and to me? My hour has not yet come," she calmly instructed the servants, "Do whatever he tells you" (John 2:3b-5). With no further word from her, Jesus provided the best wine that was served. This, the first of his signs, "revealed his glory; and his disciples believed in him" (John 2:11b). Without his mother's urging, would his glory have been revealed so soon and would his disciples have believed? It was time; his hour had come, and his mother knew it. The role that God had revealed to this woman of self-esteem had been accepted and completed. Jesus' work had begun; he was no longer her son but his Father's.

Accepting her background role and observing his ministry from a distance, Mary seemed always to be present. When she and his brothers and sisters attempted to see him when he was surrounded by a crowd, she heard him say, pointing to the crowd, "Here are my mother and my brothers! Whoever does the will of God is my brother and sister and mother" (Mark 3:34-35). Again Mary was reminded that this special child belonged to all who obeyed God. He was no longer a part of one small family. He was truly of the household of his Father.

Staying close at hand, Mary was present at the cross in those final hours. How it must have pained her to see her child suffer! Although he now belonged to the world, she had given him life, and she felt his pain. He looked at her, and loving her, gave her a new, substitute son. From the cross he instructed her to accept his beloved disciple John as her son, and at the same time he instructed John to care for his mother as if she were his own. Both were obedient to his instructions.

Mary appears one final time in the Scriptures. She was present in the upper room praying with the apostles (Acts 1:14). She and her other sons were devoted to prayer for the new church. She had raised her children well. She had fulfilled her mission. She was indeed a woman blessed and favored; she was a woman of self-esteem!

Anna

❧

She was an old woman, widowed for many years. She never left the Temple, spending all of her time praying and fasting. All she had was her faith, but that was enough, for it had provided for her a wonderful sense of self-esteem. She had married young and had hoped to have children, but her husband died after they had been married a short seven years, and she was left childless. She was well acquainted with disappointment, grief, and suffering. All that she had not personally experienced, she had observed as others had come into the temple to pray. She had prayed with and for them, for she thought enough of herself to venture out to help others. She knew that God answered prayers.

Anna has the distinction of having been the only woman in the Gospel identified as a prophet. Her years in the Temple must have attributed to this identification, for surely God had revealed things to her as a result of her faithfulness. Her ongoing connection to God through constant prayer and fasting kept hope alive in her heart and enhanced her self-esteem. Prayer and fasting were her lifelines.

She knew that the Messiah had been born, and because she never left the Temple, she was already there when Simeon and the child's parents arrived. Simeon had been promised that he would not die until he had seen the Messiah. Anna watched as Simeon's promise became a reality. He held the Messiah in his arms, and his soul rejoiced as he exclaimed, "Master, now you are dismissing your servant in peace, according to your word; for my eyes have seen your salvation, which you have prepared in the presence of all peoples, a light for revelation to the Gentiles and for glory to your people Israel" (Luke 2:29-32). Oh, how Anna's heart burned within. She too had seen the Messiah!

Anna could not contain her joy. The fulfillment of Simeon's promise had inspired her and verified her own sense of prophecy. She had to speak! "At that moment she came, and began to praise God and to speak about the child to all who were looking for the redemption of Jerusalem" (Luke 2:38). Thus Anna became the first to proclaim Jesus as the Christ, the Messiah. He would bring redemption to all seeking it, and Anna had been the first to proclaim it! *How might a person's involvement in her church enhance her self-esteem?*

The Anointing Woman

ze

*A*lthough many thought of her as a woman with a bad reputation, a sinner, she knew that she was a woman of self-esteem. As such she thought enough of herself to comfort and care for the Master. She had an alabaster jar of expensive oil. It was really the most expensive and precious thing that she had, and when she heard that the wonderful man called Jesus would be dining at the home of Simon the Pharisee, she knew what she had to do.

We can only wonder how she had purchased this expensive oil. Had she earned the money by performing sinful acts? Why had she chosen to use this oil to anoint Jesus? If she had really wanted to give it away, why didn't she just give it to the disciples? Even they knew that they could have sold it and given the money to the poor. But perhaps God had told her that Jesus would not always be with her. After all, something had made her sad; she was weeping when she entered Simon's house.

Jesus was already seated at the table when she approached him. As the tears fell from her eyes she was able to use them to wash his feet. She dried those precious feet with her lovely hair, and she continuously kissed his feet as she anointed them with the expensive oil. How she loved him! And what woman of self-esteem would refuse to offer acts of comfort to a loved one while he lived? She knew that she had sinned, but at least she would never be one to have to say, "I wish I had in some way demonstrated my love for the Master!" Others, some of whom called her a sinner, would live to wish that they had also shown their love.

Have you ever felt uncomfortable in the presence of someone who has a bad reputaiton? How is self-esteem a factor in how you related to this person? Those assembled around the table were certainly distressed to be in the company of this sinful woman, but she ignored their stares and continued in her ministrations to the Master. She did not care that their opinion of her did not change; she only wanted to do what she could while she could. She was a woman of self-esteem, for somehow she knew that what she was doing would erase a multitude of sins. She felt worthy.

As Simon watched her he began to doubt the authenticity of Jesus as a prophet of God. He said to himself, "If this man were a prophet, he would have known who and what kind of woman this is who is touching him—that she is a sinner" (Luke 7:39). Jesus, knowing Simon's thoughts and considering the attitudes of those present, was inspired to teach one of his most beautiful lessons. He said, "Simon, I have something to say to you" (Luke 7:40). Being given the permission to speak, Jesus told the parable of the creditor and the two debtors. One debtor owed the creditor ten times as much as the other one. When neither could pay, the creditor canceled both debts. Wanting Simon to carefully consider how much each debtor owed and how much each had been forgiven, Jesus asked, "Now which of them will love him more?" (Luke 7:42b). Simon was quick to respond that the one for whom the greater debt had been canceled. Jesus verified that Simon had answered correctly. Then turning to the woman, but directing his words to Simon, he said, "Do you see this woman? I entered your house; you gave me no water for my feet, but she has bathed my feet with her tears and dried them with her hair. You gave me no kiss, but from the time I came in she has not stopped kissing my feet. You did not anoint my head with oil, but she has anointed my feet with ointment. Therefore, I tell you, her sins, which were many, have been forgiven; hence she has shown great love. But the one to whom little is forgiven, loves little" (Luke 7:44-47).

The anointing woman had been correct in all of her assumptions about the Master. He was a man who would welcome her ministrations and forgive her sins. He was a man who could perceive her great love and know that she was grateful for the gift of forgiveness that only he could offer. He indeed had verified her sense of worth. She did not have to worry that she really was not welcome in Simon's house. The servant role and hospitality with which she had greeted the Lord were those that a more loving host should have shown. But because Simon was a Pharisee, an interpreter of the Law, he probably felt himself guilty of little or no sin for which to be forgiven. Therefore, he had little or no love to extend.

Jesus forgave the anointing woman all her sins and said to her, "Your faith has saved you; go in peace" (Luke 7:50). Can you imagine her joy? Jesus had accepted her love and he had forgiven her sins! He recognized her great faith that had assured her salvation. He knew her to be a woman of self-esteem. And everywhere the gospel is preached, she is remembered. Praise God!

Mary of Bethany

ᔔ

*A*lthough she lived during the first century when women could not exercise their rights to choose, she exercised a personal choice that made her a woman of self-esteem. At all times she was expected to be willing to assume the traditional role of doing the housework and preparing meals for the family's guests, but she chose to join the men and sit at the feet of Jesus in her pursuit of intellectual and spiritual growth. Her decision did not please her sister, Martha, who was left to prepare alone, but it won the support of Jesus and that was what she really cared about.

Just think. Mary of Bethany was wise enough even during the time in which she lived to realize the importance of people over things, knowledge over tasks, and spiritual nourishment over physical nourishment. The personal time she decided to take for herself to be with Jesus would make her a better person. The house would get dirty again, and the food would be eaten, and all who ate would get hungry again, but she would feast on the words of life forever. It took self-confidence and self-esteem to arrive at that kind of decision making.

We see Martha as the homemaker, who at this point in her life is probably widowed, but her sister, who may never have married, lives with her.[10] The Scripture supports this assumption by recording that "a woman named Martha welcomed him [Jesus]

---

10. Edith Deen, *All of the Women of the Bible* (San Francisco: Harper, 1988), p. 177.

into her home" (Luke 10:38). Now Mary may have truly viewed this invitation to have been made by Martha alone; therefore, she did not feel compelled to assist in the food preparations. But Martha was hurt and angry that her sister had chosen to make herself comfortable in the presence of the men while she was left alone to see to the meal. So Martha went to Jesus knowing that he would be the only one who could pry Mary away. She said, "Lord, do you not care that my sister has left me to do all the work by myself? Tell her then to help me" (Luke 10:40). Although Jesus felt Martha's frustration, he knew that the things she was worried about had no real meaning. He was on his way to Calvary and she was concerned with food. He had only a few more opportunities to teach the gospel, and she wanted someone to help her with the chores. He needed to teach, and Mary needed to listen. His response was the only one he could give, "Martha, Martha, you are worried and distracted by many things; there is need of only one thing. Mary has chosen the better part, which will not be taken away from her" (Luke 10:41-42).

All of the things that concerned Martha would pass away, but the Word of God would last forever. Mary had indeed chosen the better part. And this decision provided Jesus with another opportunity to demonstrate his inclusiveness of women in his ministry. Women gained a higher status during his lifetime. They provided for him in ways that men never even considered. They were there for him at his beginning and at his end and they followed him wherever he went. He was their champion, and they were included in his teachings.

Mary had indeed listened to and learned from Jesus, and when her brother Lazarus died, she greeted the Master with the words, "Lord, if you had been here, my brother would not have died" (John 11:32). Interestingly enough, Martha had said the same words to Jesus moments earlier while Mary was in the house weeping with friends. Even though Martha had not chosen the better part during the visit of Jesus to her home, she knew that the Master could have cured all illness and saved her brother from death. Both women were sure of the same thing. They knew that the Lord was wonderfully able to do all that was needed. *Do you think of yourself as more like Mary or more like Martha?* Whether we choose to be a Mary or a Martha, we can be people of self-esteem. Our journey toward wholeness leads us to knowledge of the Master. Jesus loved this whole family, and he loves us no matter which way we choose to serve him. Thanks be to God!

Martha

ð&

Martha was typical of the women of her time. She fully accepted the role of caretaker. She had a comfortable home and enjoyed entertaining. The fact that her sister was around to help her assured her that she would be able to do all that was required whenever guests appeared.

On one particular day the guest was Jesus. Martha wanted everything to be perfect for the Master. She wanted him to enjoy the delicious meal she was preparing and knowing that the disciples would be with him, she sought to make sure that there was enough of everything to go around. Women of self-esteem are like that. They want everything to be as perfect as possible. They often feel that the appearance of their home and their food reflects themselves, and they are very proud of all that is associated with them.

Martha just could not understand why her sister was not helping her in the preparations. She had expected Mary to be anxious to help in any way she could, but now Martha did not know how to pry her away from the feet of the Master. So, she did the only thing she could think of—she asked the Master to compel her sister to work. Martha was bold enough to speak her mind. She needed help, and she asked for it. Martha did not understand that everyone did not think her meal was as important as she did. Women of self-esteem may make this kind of mistake. If in their great confidence they view something to be important, then surely it must be. They may fail to realize that things that are high on their own agenda may not be high on the agenda of others.

Martha could not believe her ears when Jesus said, "Martha, Martha, you are worried and distracted by many things; there is need of only one thing. Mary has chosen the better part, which will not be taken away from her" (Luke 10:41-42). Why did the Master say that there was need of only one thing? There were several things that needed to be done. Martha's mind was fixed on her own previously set agenda, and she did not realize that the Master also had an agenda for his visit. She did not know that soon he would no longer be with them; she did not know that his ministry was drawing to a close; she did not know that Mary needed to spend the time to better prepare them both for the days to come. Being a woman of self-esteem, she had not stopped to consider the fact that there might actually be something better than that for which she was planning. But because she was the woman that she was, she accepted the Master's words and continued alone in the preparations and waited for the opportunity to learn from her sister all that had been said.

Martha learned well. She knew that the Master could do all things, so when her brother, Lazarus, became ill, she sent word to Jesus. She knew that he would come because she knew how much he loved her family. She also knew that somehow he would do something. Her actions were reminiscent of his mother Mary's when the wine ran out at the wedding at Cana. Somehow Mary knew that Jesus would do something. Martha knew that too. If only he would come! But Jesus did not come. Several days passed, and Lazarus died. When he did finally make it to Bethany, Martha ran to meet him speaking boldly, "Lord, if you had been here, my brother would not have died. But even now I know that God will give you whatever you ask of him" (John 11:21-22). Jesus did not respond to her as he had to his mother asking what she wanted of him, for he knew what she wanted and his time of ministry had come. Jesus simply told Martha that her brother would rise again. Being the woman that she was, faithful to the law and the prophets, Martha responded, "I know that he will rise again in the resurrection on the last day" (John 11:24). With that statement Martha became one of the first to learn the truth about Jesus and the resurrection during his lifetime and she became the first to bear witness to that truth. "Jesus said to her, 'I am the resurrection and the life. Those who believe in me, even though they die, will live, and everyone who lives and believes in me will never die. Do you believe this?' She said to him, 'Yes, Lord, I believe that you are the Messiah, the Son of God, the one coming into the world'" (John 11:25-27).

Martha had expressed her faith. Although both Martha and her sister Mary had been disappointed that Jesus had not come sooner, somehow she knew that his delay in coming was not a denial of her request. She went back to the house to get Mary who had been too disappointed to run to meet the Master. Hearing that Jesus had actually arrived, Mary went to meet him and greeted him with the same words her sister had used, letting him know that if he had been there, he could have done something.

When Jesus observed the tears of the sisters and the people who were comforting them, he thought of all the times of grief that would affect his loved ones for centuries to come, and he wept. He could and would bring Lazarus back, but what of all of those future times when he would not be there? His own death and suffering would teach them that death was not eternal.

Jesus instructed those who had gathered to roll away the stone that blocked the entrance to the tomb. But our bold Martha again spoke up saying, "Lord, already there is a stench because he has been dead four days" (John 11:39). Jesus had to remind her of that to which she had just borne witness. "Did I not tell you that if you believed, you would see the glory of God?" (John 11:40). *Have you, like Martha, ever forgotten just what you have just said you believe?* No longer resisting his instructions, Martha waited to see the glory of God revealed. Her faith was being tested; her miracle would happen, but she had to believe.

For the sake of Martha, Mary, and the others who had gathered, Jesus prayed aloud to his Father, thanking him for answering his petition. Then he called to Lazarus, and Martha was able to witness the glory of God. How thrilled this woman of self-esteem must have been when she saw her brother walk from that tomb. She knew for herself that Jesus was the resurrection and that those who believed in him, even though they had died would live again. Martha could witness to her faith for the rest of her life, and she knew that even after death she would live again. She had that blessed assurance. I thank God that we can share it with her!

The Persistent Widow

৶

Although many other works have labeled her the importunate widow, I like to call that mysterious woman used by Jesus in his parable of Luke 18:1-8, the persistent widow. Let's just take a look at the meaning of the word *importunate*. The *New Britannica-Webster Dictionary* published in 1988 defines *importunate* as "overly persistent in request or demand." This definition is probably why I do not use the word, for I do not perceive of the widow whom Jesus described as overly persistent; she was just persistent.

Let us review her situation. Although we have no reason to believe that she was any more than a fictitious woman created by Jesus to illustrate his point, she was, as described, representative of widows of her day. Although there had been a time in her life when she had had a man who could have pleaded her case for her, she was no longer in that position. She was currently a widow, a woman without a man. This status alone was enough to render her frightened and void of self-esteem. But frightened and unsure does not describe the persistent widow. She was sure about who she was, and she knew that she had been wronged. She also knew that it was the judge's responsibility to see that all wrongs were made right.

So our widow, being a woman of self-esteem, had a plan. She planned to visit the judge without ceasing. She knew that many bribed the judges and eventually got the favorable ruling they sought. Jesus knew this too, and that is probably why his words describing the judge were of one "who neither feared God nor had respect for people" (Luke 18:2). But our widow was not to be discouraged; she knew that she could prevail; she had faith in herself; she was a woman of self-esteem.

Not only did she have a plan, but she also prepared before enacting it. She had her speech ready, and she did not mince her words. She simply said, "Grant me justice against my opponent" (Luke 18:3b), and she planned to keep going to that unjust judge with that same plea until it was granted. She was bent on pursuing him, and she was going to be persistent. She had no time to worry about being protected against exploitation, for she knew that her cause was just and that she was capable of defending it. Without money for the bribe, her only hope was to beat the judge down with her persistence. And her plan worked. Persistence does get results. *What process do you use to overcome limitations that present themselves to you? Does this process regularly work for you?*

Now we can only speculate as to who her opponent was and why he or she had wronged her. We only know that whatever had happened needed to be rectified. Perhaps she had been exploited; perhaps her property had been stolen or claimed by a male in the family of her dead husband; or perhaps she had been put out of her house or even been made a servant. All we know is that her plan involved persistent pursuit and that the judge was so weary of her continually coming to him with the same plea that he granted her request. Perhaps he only granted her request to get rid of her. Some translations even imply that the widow was literally beating down the judge with her hands and fists. No matter what the actual situation was, we know that an unjust judge granted a defenseless widow justice because of her persistence.

Jesus wanted us to learn a lesson from this parable. We must be persistent in prayer. We can not afford the luxury of praying one time and then giving up. If an unrighteous judge will listen to and grant the request of a poor, defenseless widow, surely a just God will grant the requests of often unworthy but persistent children. Faithful persistence in prayer effects marvelous results. We do not have the power to demand that our wishes be granted. God is not the rabbit in our hat that we as magicians can produce at will. We must be patiently persistent, for it is God's good pleasure to grant us the kingdom.

Dr. George Buttrick writes, "God delays because the patience of the saints is the best weapon of the faith, for faith spreads in the earth as men persist for God despite all odds and against all disappointment."[11] This widow woman was the one who persisted against all odds because she was a woman of self-esteem. She was confident that God would help her persuade the judge, and Jesus uses her story to help us to understand the need for persistence in prayer. She is the persistent, not the importunate widow. Women of self-esteem are not overly anything; they are just adequately everything.

11. George Arthur Buttrick, *The Interpreter's Bible*, vol. 8 (Nashville: Abingdon Press, 1952), p. 307.

Mary Magdalene

*H*er words, "I have seen the Lord" (John 20:18), made her the first post-resurrection preacher of the gospel, and this proclamation of the revelation of God in her life is every preacher's message. Hearers must be able to see the revelation of God in the lives of those who preach the Word and in turn through the message see God for themselves. Mary Magdalene was a good preacher, for she had personally experienced the power of the resurrection. Those who heard her message wanted to see the risen Lord for themselves, and many of them did. Through her association with Jesus, she had become a woman of self-esteem.

Mary Magdalene had so much for which to be thankful. Although it does not appear that she was ever a poor woman, having been thought to be influential in Magdala, she was, however, a tormented woman. How troubled her spirit must have been, for from her "seven demons had gone out" (Luke 8:2*b*). We can only speculate as to the nature of the demons. Were they the demons of power, greed, envy, pride, jealousy, lust, and discouragement? Demons such as these cause mental and emotional anguish and stress. Or were they demons of physical pain, convulsions, and exhaustion? These demons would have prevented her from developing the joy that must have invaded her body when Jesus cast them out. So, full of joy and minus the demons, she followed him who had given her the gifts of spiritual peace, forgiveness, and self-respect. She could hold her head high in any group; she was no longer scorned as a woman possessed. Her blessed Jesus had cured her of her demon possession.

Although she and the little group of women who followed Jesus were not called to be disciples, they did contribute to his ministry. It was recorded that the women who accompanied Jesus and the disciples "provided for them out of their resources" (Luke 8:3b). Everywhere a group of women is mentioned in the presence of Jesus, Mary Magdalene heads the list. She did what she could to see that her Lord was cared for.

Just imagine her agony watching him suffer on the cross. What could she possibly do? How could she ease the suffering of one who had saved her from so much torment? This proud woman who had faced the contempt of those who had known about her demons knew that all she could do was faithfully be with her Lord. She would not leave him to suffer alone. She stood and watched knowing that he knew she was there. She was one of the last to leave the cross and the first to return to the tomb.

She did not fear the darkness as she made her way through the deserted streets early that Sunday morning. She was a woman with a mission, for once he had been placed in the tomb, she knew that the least she could do was properly prepare his body for burial. The onset of the Sabbath had prevented her from doing so earlier. Just imagine her devastation when she found no body to prepare. She could not stop the flow of tears. Where had they taken her Lord? Why was she being denied this one last thing she could do for him?

She ran to tell Peter and John, "They have taken the Lord out of the tomb, and we do not know where they have laid him" (John 20:2). Both Peter and John ran to the tomb to verify the truth of her message, and after their verification, they returned home. But Mary would not leave. She had to go back to the tomb; she had to find out what had happened.

A woman of self-esteem is like that. She wants the real answers. She will not casually accept what only appears to have happened. Mary knew for a fact that the body had been there, so someone must have taken it. She would find out who and where. Thanks to Jesus the demons had left her, so she could wait patiently at the tomb without internal torment and fear. And she would wait until there was a change in the situation. *What lessons could we learn from Mary's willingness to wait?*

Continuing to weep, she kept looking into the empty tomb hoping that somehow the body of her Lord would reappear. Then she saw the angels. Oh, how persistence is rewarded! The men had left and they missed the blessing that awaited! After telling the angels why she was weeping, she turned to see Jesus. Her tears and her distress clouded her vision so that she did not recognize him, but she heard the question this unknown man was asking and she told him that she would take her Lord away and attend to him if he would just tell her where the body was. This self-assured woman had no one to help her move a body, but she thought she could do it alone if necessary. All she needed to know was where her Lord was. She was a woman fully confident of her ability to do what needed to be done. And she was rewarded.

There is something about hearing one's name that clears one's vision. Mary had not stopped crying, and the man before her had not changed in appearance, but when he called her by her name, she recognized him. Finally knowing the man before her to be her risen Lord, Mary wanted to do what any believer would—she wanted to hold on to him forever, never letting him go. But Jesus had a mission for her. She had to go to tell others that he had risen and was ascending to his Father and their Father, his God and their God. The same God who had raised him would take care of all of them in the months and years to come. All they had to do was believe, for without the resurrection there is no Christian faith.

Mary ran with her message, "I have seen the Lord," and those who heard her knew that she had!

Dorcas

ह

*W*hen we think of biblical women of self-esteem we must consider Dorcas. Her life is simply summed up in the words, "Now in Joppa there was a disciple whose name was Tabitha, which in Greek is Dorcas. She was devoted to good works and acts of charity" (Acts 9:36). Dorcas was a disciple of Jesus Christ. She must have had self-esteem to have been a disciple, for only those who live the gospel and believe that they can make a difference in the lives of others can be disciples. And disciples are successful. Their success is measured in terms of their commitment to Jesus Christ, and Dorcas was successful.

Furthermore, Dorcas did live the gospel. She was devoted to good works and acts of charity. Dorcas was a seamstress; she made clothes for others and was known for her many acts of kindness. It would have been almost impossible for her to do good works for others if she had thought very little of herself. But Dorcas had no problem with her self-esteem, for there were many evidences of her good work and her reputation for charity was known throughout the area. Although Dorcas did not perform her works of charity for fame, sometimes we do measure success in terms of notoriety. Dorcas was well-known, but being well-known is not a criteria for success or self-esteem.

We do not know anything about Dorcas' husband, but we can assume that she was a woman of means, for she had enough to share with others. She may very well have been a widow, for no mention is made of her husband and according to the biblical account, there were a number of widows present at her home.

This further supports the fact that Dorcas was indeed somebody special. She was a disciple; she was known for her works of charity; and her friends gathered at her home when she died. In fact, upon learning of her death disciples who knew that Peter was in the area sent for him with this request, "Please come to us without delay" (Acts 9:38b). This was an urgent request deserving immediate response. The death of Dorcas was important enough to send for Peter, a disciple who had been with the Lord.

When Peter arrived, her friends showed him evidences of her many good works, the tunics and clothes she had made. They demonstrated her success and wanted him to know what a great loss she was to the Christian community. They wanted him to know that Dorcas had done something with her life. She had been a source of inspiration and support to many, for she knew she was a person of great worth. She was the Lord's disciple—her sense of self-esteem was secure. She had been something, a disciple; she had done something, acts of charity; and she had left something, handmade clothes and many friends. That's the real measure of worth. *Relate this idea to self-esteem. Is it possible to be a person of worth and not have self-esteem?*

And Peter responded. He saw that Dorcas had been a disciple; she had done something with her life; and she had left something. But her work was not finished. Peter dismissed everyone from the room and after having prayed, he woke Dorcas from the dead. What a powerful prayer that must have been! I wonder whether the widows and disciples who had sent for Peter expected him to restore their friend to them. We may never know, but we do know that Dorcas became a source of evangelism. The Scripture records that news of her restoration to life became known throughout the region and "many believed in the Lord" (Acts 9:42b).

Mary, John Mark's Mother

৵

*J*ohn Mark's mother is one of six women named Mary in the New Testament. The other five are the mother of Jesus, the mother of James and Joses, Mary of Bethany, Mary Magdalene, and Mary of Rome. All six were loving and faithful women, and all were either instrumental in the life of Jesus or in the building of the early Church. I have already identified three of these Marys (Mary the mother of Jesus, Mary of Bethany, and Mary Magdalene) as women of self-esteem. John Mark's mother is the fourth.

She was a woman of considerable means, having a house big enough to entertain the many Christians who frequently assembled for prayer. She was also wealthy enough to have maids, one of whom was Rhoda. Mary was one of the women blessed to have had a child, but at the time of her early church leadership, she was probably a widow. The properties mentioned in the New Testament writings were identified as belonging to her, and no mention of a husband is made.

There always seemed to be prayer going on at her house, and at the time that Peter was jailed, Mary led those who gathered in prayer for his safety. The early church members were especially concerned about Peter, for Herod had already killed James, the brother of John, and this action seemed to have pleased the Jews. Peter was being held under tight security because it was feared that he would attempt an escape. "While Peter was kept in prison, the church [at Mary's house] prayed fervently to God for him" (Acts 12:5).

God heard their prayers and Peter miraculously escaped. His chains dropped, and he was led from the jail by an angel of the Lord. He went straight to the house of Mary "where many had gathered and were praying" (Acts 12:12*b*). Mary knew how to conduct a prayer meeting, and while she and the others continued in prayer, her maid, Rhoda, went to answer the knock at the door.

Rhoda was so shocked to see Peter that she closed the door without admitting him and ran to tell the others that he was out of jail and present with them. Of course, they thought she was mad. But Rhoda had her own sense of self-esteem. She had enough faith in herself and in who she had seen at the door to defy those who doubted her and insist that what she said was indeed true.

Peter continued to knock, having not yet been admitted, and finally someone opened the door. The proud and willing servant, Rhoda, served him and her mistress although the hour was late, and Peter gave instructions to the faithful who were gathered.

Mary must have been thrilled that Peter had come straight to her home after experiencing the presence of an angel of the Lord. Her home was a center of Christian worship in that community, and Peter could have gone nowhere else. John Mark had grown up in that Christian home, and he eventually became Peter's companion and one of the gospel writers. He was also the probable founder of the church in Alexandria.[12] How proud Mary must have been of her son who continued so competently the work of the church that she had started in her home!

Mary's influence was felt by other relatives. She was either the aunt or cousin to Barnabas (Colossians 4:10) who was both an outstanding early church leader and a companion to Paul on his first missionary journey. And all of us should feel Mary's influence knowing that the power of prayer can effect miracles. She was indeed a woman of self-esteem! *Must a person have self-esteem to be a positive influence in the lives of others?*

---

12. Edith Deen, *All of the Women of the Bible* (San Francisco: HarperSanFrancisco, 1988), p. 212.

Lydia

ঽৡ

*L*ydia was a dealer in purple cloth, cloth the color of royalty; yet, she did not feel royal. She was one of the most successful businesswomen in Philippi; yet, there was something missing from her life. She was a Gentile; yet, she would steal away in prayer to worship the God of the Jews on the Sabbath. In other words, she did not become a woman of self-esteem until she had that unique experience that made her Europe's first convert to Christianity. Becoming a disciple of Jesus Christ made her life complete. How wonderful it must have been to be the first one in Europe to become a Christian! Her Christian experience made her true royalty. At last her occupation of dealing in the royal color fit her own identity.

Lydia had always had that warm and winning personality. After all, she was successful in selling, and the dye used for the purple had to be gathered very meticulously and was therefore very expensive. So Lydia, whose personal name was the same as that of her native Asia Minor province, was a welcome and distinguished addition to the group of women who were accustomed to meeting by the river bank at Philippi for prayer on the Sabbath.

When Paul and Silas arrived at the Philippian port, they went searching for anyone who might be meeting by the river bank. It was well known that wherever there was no synagogue, worshipers met by the river. The women at Philippi were faithful in their prayer meeting, and when Paul found them, he knew that they needed to hear the word preached. Lydia was among them, and as Paul preached, the "Lord opened her heart to listen eagerly" to what he said (Acts 16:14*b*). She and all her household were baptized. The very fact that her conversion led to the conversion and baptism of the others in her household testifies to her status as a leader.

Because Lydia was a woman who had always boldly led in all of her endeavors, she was not content to take a backseat in her new faith. She wanted her home to be a focal point, and she wanted Paul and Silas to accept the hospitality she extended. She said, "If you have judged me to be faithful to the Lord, come and stay at my home" (Acts 16:15*b*). As a woman of newly found self-esteem, she prevailed upon them. Their acceptance of her invitation heightened her sense of self-worth.

Lydia's house became the first meeting place of Christians in Europe. The members of this church at Philippi were loved by Paul and were referred to as his "joy and crown" (Philippians 4:1). Perhaps they were so special to him because it was while they were in Philippi that Paul and Silas were jailed for curing a demented girl. But this incarceration was special, for it provided a setting for a dramatic demonstration of the power of the Holy Spirit. While Paul and Silas prayed and sang, God sent an earthquake to unlock the jail and loose their chains. The jailer and his whole household were subsequently converted, and Paul and Silas returned to Lydia's home. I am sure that they found Lydia and the church at Philippi in prayer for their release.

Lydia was a businesswoman. Lydia was a leader. Lydia was a Gentile who became Europe's first convert. Lydia used her business and leadership skills to build the church at Philippi. She was a woman of self-esteem! *Do you ever feel that, despite all your talents and abilities, something is missing from you life? What do you do then?*

Priscilla

ॐ

*C*onsidering the times in which Priscilla lived, she had to have been a woman of self-esteem. We know that she was married, for she and her husband are mentioned several times, and interestingly enough, Priscilla's name is mentioned first most of the time. This recording of facts about them, especially with her name appearing first, validates our assumption that she was indeed an important and influential woman.

Priscilla was a partner with her husband in the art of tentmaking and as such it was natural that the apostle Paul, also a tentmaker, would identify with them. Priscilla and her husband Aquila often extended their hospitality to Paul whenever he was in Corinth, and their arrangement proved beneficial to all. When the Roman emperor, Claudius, expelled all the Jews from Italy, Priscilla and Aquila ended up in Corinth. Not only did Paul stay with them, but he also invited them to accompany him on his missionary journey to Ephesus. So Priscilla became one of the first female missionaries.

But Priscilla was more than a wife and missionary; she was also a teacher of the gospel of Jesus Christ. She became instrumental in teaching the brilliant Old Testament scholar Apollos, who had been exposed to the teachings of Jesus but knew only the baptism of John. In other words, he knew about baptism by the water but not by the Holy Spirit. Apollos was an enthusiastic preacher and spoke boldly concerning the way of the Lord, but Priscilla and Aquila "took him aside and explained the Way of God to him more accurately" (Acts 18:26*b*). *Would you* *be confident enough to presume to instruct "more accurately" about your faith to an acclaimed scholar?* She had to have self-esteem to challenge his theology. But she also knew that with his background Apollos would be a great help in convincing the Jews through Old Testament scripture that Jesus was indeed the long-awaited Messiah. She felt called to help him know and understand Jesus as more than a historical figure. He had to know Jesus as his personal Savior, a living spirit in his personal life; he had to personally know and feel the power of the Holy Spirit. That was the task that Priscilla undertook, and once accomplished there was a new power in the preaching of the eloquent Apollos. The presence of the Holy Spirit could be felt. Priscilla is indeed an example of the way God uses the talents of teachers to enhance the gifts of their students.

The homes that Priscilla and Aquila established in both Corinth and Ephesus became the local churches. People came from the surrounding areas to learn more about the gospel. Paul left them in Ephesus knowing that the work of the Master was in good hands. When he returned he found the church thriving. Priscilla and Aquila had been good stewards of the task of kingdom building. After the death of Emperor Claudius, they returned to Rome to establish a church in their home there. What a blessing it was that they were obviously wealthy enough to sponsor churches and entertain students and leaders in their various homes.

Priscilla's prominence and central position in the early history of the church is remembered with monuments, catacombs, and churches bearing her name. She was a dedicated servant of Jesus Christ. She was a woman of self-esteem.

Phoebe

ॐ

She was from Cenchreae, a port of Corinth, and she traveled to Rome carrying Paul's letter to the Romans. She was respected and trusted by Paul and the letter she bore served as her introduction to the church at Rome.

Her name was Phoebe, and Paul described her as a "sister," a "deacon," one who should be welcomed "in the Lord as is fitting for the saints" (Romans 16:1-2). Paul's introduction was high praise. He had taken the time to let the church know that Phoebe was a member of the family of God; she was a sister. She was more than a bench member of the church at Cenchreae, she was a leader, a deacon. She might even have been the preacher. Paul also cautioned the Romans to greet and welcome her as one would welcome a saint and as saints should welcome one another. This greeting alone would certainly have been a source of Phoebe's self-esteem.

Paul continued his introduction of his sister and friend by soliciting help for her "in whatever she may require from you, for she has been a benefactor of many and of myself as well" (Romans 16:2*b*). Phoebe must have been a woman of wealth and power, for she was in a position to help the church at Rome as she had helped so many others, including Paul himself. Paul had personal knowledge of her ability to benefit others, but he was aware that even those in a position to help the early church needed the cooperation of the church members. Paul wanted the Romans to know that this woman was worthy of their support. *Imagine then as now that women were often rejected as persons* *of leadership and power. How would you keep going? How is your self-esteem a factor?* Thank God that in Paul Phoebe had a respected ally.

Phoebe had traveled alone, and no mention is made of family members. Her family was the church. Her home had been open to the Christians in Cenchreae, and she obviously had the means of supporting and providing for all who sought refuge there. Like Lydia and Priscilla, she had been a woman who had shown early Christians considerable hospitality. She had left whatever security she had at home seeking the same hospitality she had so often extended. She was on a mission to Rome for Paul, and through his introduction, he had tried to make sure that she was accepted.

What a wonderful person she must have been! What a valuable work she must have performed to have been so highly recommended. Paul had extoled her virtue and her contributions. He was not hesitant about expressing his view of her as a woman worthy of great respect. He saw her as a woman of self-esteem. I am sure that she was!

*C*onclusion

"I thought I could; I thought I could!"

ॐ

*I*n my estimation each of the biblical women I have discussed thought she could. Each was a woman of confidence, faith, and determination. She was not importunate, overly anything; she was just adequately everything she needed to be for the situation in which she found herself. She was God's instrument, and she used the gifts and graces she had to accomplish what God intended. Because she was a woman of self-esteem, she knew that where her strength and ability ended, God's was simply beginning. How could she fail?

She had to rely on her revelation of the will of God, and that is what each woman, whether in biblical or modern times, must do. Others may not agree with her actions, but a woman of self-esteem must do what she believes is right. In the case of Eve, she was disobedient, for she had no history of the faith of her fathers and mothers on which to draw. She made the mistake of believing that she could be as knowledgeable as God once she had eaten of the tree of the knowledge of good and evil. But painfully Eve learned that she was not equal to God, and her lesson did not have to be repeated by those women who followed.

Jael and Judith believed that the violent acts they committed were within the will of God, and I agree with them. Vengeance is God's, and these women were used to effect it. But most of the women I selected were women of faith. They were women of self-esteem because of their unique relationship and commitment to God. They really believed that they could be the vehicles of the will of God. Like Esther they saved nations; like Jehoshabeath they preserved kings; like Mary Magdalene they preached the gospel; and like Dorcas they became disciples. They never considered their limitations; they just counted on their abilities. They believed in themselves and they believed in their God. They knew that they were valuable persons of worth, and they just thought that they could.

As each woman accomplished her task and lived the life God had revealed to her, she could proudly say, "I thought I could; I thought I could." Yes! She just thought she could and she did. Hallelujah!

*B*ibliography

Auld, A. Graeme. *Joshua, Judges, and Ruth.* Philadelphia: Westminster Press, 1984.

———. First and Second Kings. Philadelphia: Westminster Press, 1986.

Barclay, William. *The Acts of the Apostles.* Philadelphia: Westminster Press, 1976.

——— *The Gospel of Luke.* Philadelphia: Westminster Press, 1975.

——— *The Gospel of Matthew,* vols. 1 and 2. Philadelphia: Westminster Press, 1975.

——— *The Gospel of Mark.* Philadelphia: Westminster Press, 1975.

——— *The Letter to the Romans.* Philadelphia: Westminster Press, 1975.

Barker, William P. *Everyone in the Bible.* Westwood: Fleming H. Revell Company, 1966.

Berquist, Jon L. *Reclaiming Her Story.* St. Louis: Chalice Press, 1992.

Cunningham, Sarah. *We Belong Together: Churches in Solidarity with Women.* New York: Friendship Press, 1992.

Deen, Edith. *All of the Women of the Bible.* San Francisco: Harper, 1988.

Ellison, H. L. *Exodus.* Philadelphia: Westminster Press, 1982.

Fish, Becky Durost. "When Change Transforms Our Lives." *365 More Meditations for Women.* Nashville: Abingdon Press, 1992.

Gibson, John C. L. *Genesis.* vols. 1 and 2. Louisville: Westminster Press, 1981-82.

McConville, J. G. *Ezra, Nehemiah, and Esther.* Philadelphia: Westminster Press, 1985.

Millett, Craig Ballard. *In God's Image.* San Diego: LuraMedia, 1991.

Newsom, Carol A. and Ringe, Sharon H. *The Women's Bible Commentary.* Louisville: Westminster/John Knox Press, 1992.

Payne, David F. *First and Second Samuel* Philadelphia: Westminster Press, 1982.

Piper, Watty. *The Little Engine That Could.* New York: Platt and Munk, 1961.

Plaut, W. Gunther. *The Torah.* New York: Union of American Hebrew Congregations, 1981.

Riggins, Walter. *Numbers.* Philadelphia: Westminster Press, 1983.

Sanford, Linda T. and Donovan, Mary Ellen. *Women and Self-Esteem.* New York: Penguin Books, 1985.

Weems, Renita J. *Just a Sister Away.* San Diego: LuraMedia, 1988.

Winter, Miriam Therese. *The Gospel According to Mary.* New York: Crossroad, 1993.

Zimmer, Mary. *Sister Images.* Nashville: Abingdon Press, 1993.

I_{ndex}